Emerging Medieval Europe

BORZOI STUDIES IN HISTORY

Consulting Editor:

EUGENE RICE

Columbia University

Archibald R. Lewis

THE UNIVERSITY OF TEXAS

Emerging Medieval Europe, A.D. 400-1000

Alfred · A · Knopf • NEW YORK

FIRST PRINTING

Library of Congress Catalog Card Number: 67–10713
Manufactured in the United States of America.

⋖ Contents ⋗

INTRODUCTION   ix

chapters

I. *The Empire and the Barbarians,*
    A.D. 400–565   3
    THE SHIFTING BALANCE   5
    PROBLEMS OF POLITICAL POWER   7
    THE ECONOMIC SPHERE   11
    SOCIAL RELATIONS AND
        INTERRELATIONS   22
    THE CHURCH   25
    CULTURAL LIFE   31
    SUMMARY   37

II. *Monks and Warriors,* A.D. 565–718   39
    THE GREAT POWERS   41
    ECONOMIC DEVELOPMENTS   47
    SOCIAL DEVELOPMENTS EAST AND WEST   58
    RELIGIOUS CHANGES   61
    CULTURAL PROGRESS   67
    SUMMARY   74

chapters

III. *The Carolingian Era*, A.D. 718–840   76

EMERGENCE OF THE
CAROLINGIAN EMPIRE   77
THE BYZANTINE EMPIRE   84
ECONOMIC CHANGES   87
RELATIONS WITH THE CHURCH   99
CULTURAL LIFE   103

IV. *The Age of the Vikings,*
A.D. 840–911   110

AN AGE OF INVASIONS   111
POLITICAL REPERCUSSIONS   116
SOCIAL AND ECONOMIC IMPACT   120

V. *A New Europe*, A.D. 911–1000   136

POLITICAL DIVISIONS OF EUROPE   137
ECONOMIC PROGRESS   147
THE SOCIAL SPHERE   154
THE PROGRESS OF LEARNING   160
ARCHITECTURE AND CREATIVITY   163

CONCLUSION   165

SUGGESTIONS
FOR FURTHER READING   168

INDEX   *follows page* 170

❧ Maps ❧

1. *Europe about* A.D. 400   18

2. *Europe about* A.D. 630   52

3. *Europe about* A.D. 820   94

4. *Europe about* A.D. 1000   148

⋅⋲ *Introduction* ⋺⋅

T he initial problem that faces any scholar who attempts to deal with the early medieval history of Europe is that of deciding just what the term "Europe" really means. The traditional answer has been to view Europe as a rather restricted area. Scholars who hold such a view begin by agreeing that the Roman Empire, at least in the West, was European. Once the Barbarians have taken over this area, however, these historians consistently restrict the scope of what they regard as European to the Carolingian Empire and to a few borderlands, such as the British Isles, Scandinavia, and Western Slavdom. The Byzantine Empire, the Spain that was occupied by the Moslems, and most of Slavic Europe seem to lie beyond their ken.

In this volume, a quite different view is taken. Europe is regarded as including the entire European continent that lies north of Africa and west of Asia, from the Urals to the Atlantic. Throughout this book, then, a good part of the Byzantine Empire, as well as Moslem Spain and Russia are regarded as part of European medieval history. This has its obvious hazards. On the other hand, it avoids the inconsistency of including Visigothic Spain in Europe, and excluding the emirate of Cordova. It refuses to overlook Byzantine territory in Italy, while considering Theodoric's kingdom as somehow European. It adds on to Europe those vast stretches of territory that the Slavs inhabited, instead of slighting them in favor of the more westerly Germans. In short, it attempts to bring a new dimension and breadth to this period of European development. If this results in new perspectives, the effort may well be worthwhile.

There is a second reason for writing such a book as this. For a long time, historians, along with the educated public generally, were content to dismiss early medieval history as hardly worth serious study. In recent years, however, a very different view of these centuries has emerged. To the limited literary sources that have survived, we can now add fresh insights derived from the spade of the archeologist, the analyses of the numismatist, and the researches of the art historian and the historian of technology. Nor are we any longer content to dismiss any period as merely primitive or barbaric. An era like our own, whose artists have been vitally affected by the primitive art of Africa, Asia, and Oceania, cannot help but see merit in similar artistic works from Celtic Ireland, Anglo-Saxon England, and Vendel Sweden. And who can fail to note the similarity between Byzantine and Carolingian art and that which is being produced by contemporary artists? An age whose art is so akin to our own cannot fail to evoke our interest.

The study of the early Middle Ages is particularly relevant today in still another way. We live in a postcolonial world of painfully emerging peoples in much of Africa, Asia, and Latin America. To understand these peoples and the forces that move them, what better example is there than early medieval Europe, which over several centuries emerged out of a combination of barbarism and decayed Roman colonialism to form a new and vital civilization? To understand the emerging Europe of this period may help us to grasp at least some of the forces at work in countries like Ghana, Malaysia, or Bolivia.

Last of all, a study of the early Middle Ages in Europe helps us to understand our own Western culture. Without underestimating the extent to which we are indebted to the Hebrews, the Greeks, and the Romans, we must keep in mind that the heritage of the ancient world came to us filtered through a medieval frame of reference, which changed it and gave it a special emphasis. The early Middle Ages, then, were the seedbed out of which our modern Western world emerged; to understand them is to grasp the richness of our own special heritage.

Thus we are confronted in this period with a challenging emergent culture. From it we can learn a little about what is going on among the post-colonial peoples of our modern world; by studying it, we can also enrich our understanding of our own unique heritage. The author can only hope that this volume may help in some measure to do all these things.

Finally, the author wishes to add a special word of thanks to Professor Geoffrey Barraclough for his assistance in revising this volume for final publication. All the errors are the author's, but without Professor Barraclough's suggestions they would be much more numerous.

Austin, Texas   A.R.L.
October, 1966

Emerging Medieval Europe

chapter I

The Empire and the Barbarians, A.D. 400–565

*A*s the fourth century ended, a few short years after the death of the Emperor Theodosius, the area that was to become the Europe of later times presented a curious picture. It was a Europe that seemed, at first glance, to be separated into distinct Roman and barbarian worlds. The division between these two Europes had existed for some four centuries, ever since the time of Augustus. Roman Europe stretched south and west of the Rhine-Danube frontier to the Mediterranean and the Atlantic; it had one extension, Roman Britain, to the north. The rest of the continent —Ireland, Scotland, Scandinavia, most of Germany, eastern Europe, and Russia—belonged to an assortment of barbarian peoples.

Roman Europe was divided into provinces, which a well-organized bureaucracy governed for its emperors. It possessed a highly developed system of written Roman law, and was officially subject to a well-defined orthodox Christianity. It was defended by an organized Roman army, which for centuries had had as its main objective the defense of its frontiers. It had a common gold and silver coinage, and a network of roads that facilitated commerce. It was subject to onerous taxation to support its army and its officials. Its upper classes lived either in towns or cities, or else in large villas which, like early twentieth-century plantations in Africa and Asia, formed self-sufficient units in the countryside. It had a common Orientalized and Christianized Greco-Roman civilization, which it shared with those parts of the Empire that lay to the south and east of it, along the African and Asian shores of the Mediterranean.

Barbarian Europe was much more formless. It was made up not of provinces but of tribes, some of which had combined into large confederacies. These tribes were often migratory, so that the boundaries that separated them were unstable. Law in the Roman sense hardly existed beyond the Empire's borders, for that which the barbarian peoples followed was personal, tribal, and customary. While the Barbarians were warlike, they were led by war chiefs who had little grasp of the kind of military organization that had long prevailed within the Empire. No roads existed to encourage commerce; gold and silver, although they were in use, had not yet replaced more primitive methods of economic exchange. There were no taxes, in the Roman sense, beyond the Empire's frontiers, and religious life lacked the characteristic Roman uniformity. Most barbarian peoples were pagan; those that were Christian had adopted a heretical brand of Arian Christianity that had died out within the Empire. Barbarian Europe possessed no towns, and nothing like the well-organized

Roman villa system. Nor did its peoples share at all in the Christianized Greco-Roman civilization that still united the upper classes of the Roman Empire.

The Shifting Balance

THE DECLINING ROMAN EMPIRE

One can overemphasize, however, the contrast between these two worlds—Roman and barbarian—especially at the end of the fourth century. Parts of the Roman Empire were less civilized than one often assumes. Tribalism remained the rule in such regions as northwestern Spain, northern and western Britain, and the Balkans. Barbarian *foederati*, as allied groups of Germans were called, such as the Visigoths and some of the Franks and Alemanni, were already settled within the Empire's borders. The Christianization of the population that lived in such tribal areas was superficial, as it was in much of the Roman countryside; the word "pagan," derived from *paganus*, or country dweller, shows this clearly.

The Roman army, especially in the West, was now almost completely barbarian. It was led by generals of barbarian origin, who commanded the same sort of personal loyalty from their troops that we find in war-bands on the other side of the frontier. The tactics of this army had also changed from those once used by Rome's older and more disciplined legions. Now its elite troops, mounted on horses, charged into battle, as did their barbarian opponents. Although gold and silver money was used by the upper classes, the mass of inhabitants in the Roman countryside were state serfs, called *coloni*, who were bound to the soil and employed an economy in kind, distinctly local in character, and not too different from that found beyond the Roman frontiers.

Foederati within the Empire were perhaps already using their own laws instead of the Roman legal system, which may be the reason why the Visigoths, after they crossed the Danube, objected to having Roman administration forced upon them. We know that by the year 400 the Empire's taxation system had broken down in many parts of the West, as large landowners evaded its imposts and helped their dependents do the same. Towns had been declining in many areas since the third century, and in some frontier regions the once prosperous villas had all but disappeared. Even the Greco-Roman culture of the upper classes, now diluted by Orientalization, was weakening, and pre-Roman art forms were reappearing in parts of Britain, Gaul, and Spain. A declining Roman Empire in Europe was moving away from the common destiny that had long linked it to Roman North Africa and Asia.

CHANGES IN BARBARIAN EUROPE

By the year 400, moreover, centuries of contact with a more civilized Roman world had so altered barbarian Europe that the contrast between it and what had long been Roman was already blurred. As the Roman world became more barbarian, the barbarian world became more civilized. During the fourth century, for instance, Ireland not only borrowed some of the material elements of Roman civilization, it was also affected by Christianity. Across the Rhine–Danube frontiers, great confederacies under hereditary kings had replaced the small tribal groupings of Caesar's and Tacitus' time. Many of the free western Germans, who had earlier been nomadic, now lived a settled agricultural life and tilled the soil with heavy wheeled ploughs, superior to those used in Roman Mediterranean regions. Some eastern German peoples were already Christian by the year 400, as a result of the efforts of such Arian missionaries as Ulfilas. Even distant Scandinavia had been so affected by its contacts with Rome that modern archeologists refer to this period as the Roman Iron Age in Scandinavia. By the fourth century, this Roman influence was being challenged by new ones that originated in part from Central Asia and Sassanian Persia, but this was also true of regions within the Empire itself. It seems fair to say, then, that by 400 the line separating Roman and Barbarian had become blurred. This foreshadowed the end of the division between them, which was to take place in the next century and a half, during what are usually referred to as the barbarian invasions.

Problems of Political Power

Between 400 and 565, Europe was affected by a series of dramatic changes. As far as Roman Europe is concerned, one can divide this era into two periods. The first saw the collapse of the entire Western Empire and the appearance in its place of a number of barbarian kingdoms: Visigothic, Ostrogothic, Burgundian, Frankish, Suevian, Vandal, and Anglo-Saxon—a process that had been largely completed by the year 500. The second period saw a resurgence of Roman power, directed from Constantinople. By 565, the year of Justinian's death, this had resulted in the Empire's recovery of North Africa, Italy, southern Spain, and the islands of the Mediterranean that had been in barbarian hands; moreover, a new revived Romania had appeared in the western Mediterranean—a fact that was to affect Europe profoundly.

MOVEMENTS OF BARBARIAN PEOPLES

Beyond what had long been the Roman frontiers in Europe, equally important changes had been taking place during these years. These took the form of a series of movements of barbarian peoples. In part, these were German in character, as tribes moved south and west into the Roman world. Most of these tribes came from eastern Germany and Scandinavia, and the kingdoms they established in the Roman world were far distant from their original homes. A few of them, such as the Franks, the Alemanni, and the Saxons, on the other hand, were west Germans, who moved only a short distance across the frontiers and were thus able to keep strong connections with their homelands. By 565 this German migration had ended, except for one tribe, the Lombards, who were to cross the Alps into Italy immediately following Justinian's death.

As German tribes moved south and west, Slavic peoples followed on their heels to take over much of the territory they had vacated. Some pressed west into eastern Germany; by 565, they had reached the Elbe–Saale line, thus separating the Germans of Scandinavia from those to the south. Others, under Avar impetus, moved into Bohemia and south into the Balkans, to begin a transformation of this part of Europe down to the Peloponnesus into a Slavic-speaking region, and to come into direct contact with the Roman Empire.

Still a third movement was that which saw a number of nomadic peoples of Central Asia traverse the steppelands from southern Russia to as far west as the plains of Hungary. The Huns formed the vanguard of this movement; they were followed by the Avars, with the Bulgars and Magyars, who settled in south Russia, forming the rear echelons. By the late sixth century, the effects of this movement began the separation of the Slavs of northern and central Europe from those of the Balkans, as a belt of Turkish and Finno-Ugric-speaking nomads settled in territory that stretched from Austria to the Caspian.

NEW POLITICAL PATTERNS

When this movement of peoples had ended, a new Europe had emerged; its political and cultural character needs careful examination. The most important European power was still the Roman Empire, but it was a Rome that now exercised its authority from Constantinople. This Empire controlled Italy, the Balkans, the islands of the Mediterranean, and southern Spain. It had mustered sufficient power to destroy the ephemeral barbarian kingdoms of the Vandals and Ostrogoths. Its main strength, however, now came from its non-European provinces of Asia Minor, Syria, and Egypt. By this time, too, it was losing its Latin character and becoming essentially Greek. Nor did it any longer rely for defense exclusively on its army: rather, it had become an Empire that based its fighting power on a navy, and relied on the use of money and diplomacy to defend its borders.

The second most important power was a semi-barbarian one that came to dominate Gaul and most of western Germany during this period—the kingdom of the Franks. This kingdom emerged late in the fifth century, after the Western Roman Empire had disappeared. It was the creation of Clovis, a chieftain who united the Franks in what today is northern France, by leading them to victory over the last independent sub-Roman kingdom in Gaul, that of Sygarius. Then he subdued his rivals, the Alemanni, in the Upper Rhine region, and drove the Visigoths out of Aquitaine. During the last years of his life, he conquered the Franks of the Rhinelands and added their lands to his state. His immediate successors, although they quarreled bitterly among themselves, still managed to crush the Burgundians and annex their kingdom, to pick up Provence from the Ostrogoths, to intervene in Italy, and to establish nominal control over Bavaria and eastern Germany. By 565 their half-Roman, half-German kingdom was the strongest in western Europe.

Two other states deserve mention besides that of the Franks. One was the kingdom of the Visigoths. Driven out of all of Gaul, except Septimania, by the Franks, the Visigoths were beginning by 565 to find a new destiny in Spain. They were gradually conquering most of the peninsula from their new capital of Toledo, and developing sufficient strength to make themselves serious rivals of the Franks. The other important state was one that the Avars were beginning to form in Central Europe on the plains of Hungary during the mid-sixth century. This kingdom, like that of the Huns, was a nomadic one, in which the Avars, as a ruling minority, dominated weaker Slavic neighbors. The result was a formidable fighting force that drove the Lombards south into Italy and raided eastern Roman territory south of the Danube.

When we survey other areas of Europe, however, beyond the boundaries of the Roman Empire and the domains of the Franks, Visigoths, and Avars, we find none that had, as yet, developed much political cohesion. In the British Isles, Celts and Anglo-Saxons were just beginning to fashion kingdoms. Scandinavia seems to have been politically formless, while, except for the rather shadowy empire of the Antas, eastern Europe remained tribal. From the Elbe to the Urals and from the Carpathians to the Arctic, barbarian Europe still held sway.

The Economic Sphere

DEMOGRAPHIC CHANGES

As drastic changes took place in the political pattern of Europe, so did others in the economic and social sphere. Some were demographic changes, to which we have already alluded. These began even before the year 400, when an underpopulated Empire welcomed the entry of considerable numbers of German barbarians as individual soldiers, or *laeti*, and even as whole peoples.

When the Western Empire collapsed, such movements swelled to a flood, and large numbers of Germans moved across the old frontiers during the course of the fifth century. Entire peoples, such as the Vandals, Ostrogoths, Visigoths, and Burgundians, settled on Roman soil. Some were few in number, while others —for example, the Ostrogoths and Visigoths—may have numbered up to 300,000 in all. These Germanic peoples settled in regions that contained a large Romanized population. On the other hand, the Franks seem to have initially colonized relatively vacant lands in northern France, Belgium, and the Rhinelands, as did the Alemanni in Alsace. Only after Clovis had conquered most of Gaul did they move into more populated regions, where they may have come to form as much as 25 percent of the population in some areas.

Across the Channel in Britain, colonization by the Saxons and the Angles seems to have been a more thorough affair. They took over many areas completely, although in some regions a considerable residual Celtic population remained, and was only gradually absorbed. West Britain, consisting of Cornwall, Wales, and Strathclyde, remained solidly Celtic, however, and even provided some surplus population that crossed into Brittany. One should also note a few other population shifts in western Europe, such as Basques settling in the Garonne valley, and Scots from Ireland moving into Dalraida in Scotland.

To these movements of peoples into Roman territory we should also add another fact of great demographic importance—disease. In the sixth century, the Mediterranean world was swept by bubonic plague, which reached this area from the Far East. The results of this were momentous, particularly in Constantinople, the Balkans, and Italy, where much of the urban population was swept away. It seems probable that it is this depopulation that explains why so little resistance was encountered after 565, when the Slavs entered the Balkans in force and the Lombards did the same thing in Italy.

Dramatic as such population movements were in former Roman territory, others, almost as important, took place beyond the Rhine. Some of them have already been mentioned. Swedes moved southwest from the Uppsala region to take up lands the Angles had left vacant, while a massive Slavic migration to the west reached the Elbe-Saale line, to replace German tribes who had moved into former Roman territory. Other Slavs, impelled by the Avars, moved in force into the Balkans and some even settled in the Peloponnesus, while the Avars themselves made their homes in the Hungarian plain.

Such population movements greatly affected the future of Europe. To them the continent owes much of its present population and the distribution of its language groups. They made Britain, Scotland, Flanders, and the Rhinelands German-speaking regions. To them Czechoslovakia and the Balkans owe their Slavic character, and eastern Germany its Slavic substratum. It was also during this period that Brittany became Celtic, and Gascony Basque.

Nevertheless, these migrations affected the population of Europe at that time less than one might at first expect. Few Romans were displaced by invading Visigoths, Ostrogoths, Burgundians, or Franks, who were spread out thin as conquerors or else settled on vacant lands that belonged to the Imperial government and were known as the *fisc*. Others—for example, the Slavs in eastern Germany, the Franks in Flanders, or the Anglo-Saxons in Britain—colonized lands that were relatively denuded of population. So much of Europe, both inside and outside the old borders of the Roman Empire, was still, thanks in part to plague and depopulation, a waste of underpopulated forest, marsh, and brush that there was ample room for the newcomers to settle any region without disturbing the existing population. The main result of migrations, then, was to bring into many regions a new population that was eventually to make the lands they settled more productive than they had earlier been.

PATTERNS OF URBAN DEVELOPMENT

Other changes of an economic and social nature took place, however, that had more immediate effects. One of the more important was a change in the pattern of European urban development. As we have already noted, non-Roman Europe was not urbanized prior to the year 400, although geography dictated the emergence of certain places where trade centered and products were exchanged on a seasonal basis. Within the Empire's borders, however, a different situation prevailed. Here two quite different types of towns had developed. One consisted of urban centers near the Roman frontiers; these towns were partly administrative and also traded with the barbarian world. Their main economic function, however, was to produce the arms, cloth, and other supplies that were needed by the Roman troops who were defending the Empire's borders. As that administrative manual of the Late Empire, the *Notitia Dignitatum*, and the Theodosian Code (the mid-fifth-century Roman legal code) make clear, during this period such production was under strict governmental control. These urban centers, then, were not economically organic, but the result of the Roman government's political and military policies.

Roman towns of a quite different sort also existed, however; these were located nearer the Mediterranean, far from the Empire's frontiers. Although these urban centers had administrative functions, their chief economic role was to serve their local regions through the production, sale, and distribution of goods. While towns of this sort were certainly less prosperous by the late fourth century than had earlier been the case, as the result of governmental regimentation and the competition from villa industries, they nevertheless still continued to exist.

As the Western Empire collapsed during the course of the fifth century, towns of the type we first described tended to disappear. Their industrial production was no longer needed, since there were no longer troops to use it. The administrative system they had served no longer existed, and trade could now freely cross frontiers that had ceased to have any meaning. The process, however, was a slow one. It began to affect towns in Britain during the last decades of the fourth century, and those near the Rhine frontier, in northern France, Belgium, and the Rhinelands, during the course of the fifth. By the first decades of the sixth century, it had caused a disappearance of urban centers along the upper and middle Danube, although those along the lower Danube lingered on for another half century. By 565, the process was all but complete; towns had disappeared in a wide area close to Rome's old frontiers from Britain to the Black Sea, when they lost their economic reasons for existence.

In the same parts of Europe, we find a very similar decay of villas taking place, although the process probably took a little while longer. In many regions near the frontiers, such villas were more than agrarian centers; they were production centers for manufactured goods— rural factories, if you will. They depended for their labor force upon the use of serflike coloni, who were tied to the soil by Imperial enactment, to furnish the taxes and the labor that the Empire needed in order to defend itself. Thus, when the Empire collapsed in the West, no force existed to keep the coloni at their tasks, nor was it possible to dispose of the goods they were producing. Villas therefore had to be abandoned and gradually disappeared, just as today plantations have been disappearing in Indonesia or the Congo, where the colonial system that made them possible has since ceased to exist.

In Roman Britain, most such villas were no longer in existence by the late fourth century, although a few lingered on near Saxon Shore forts and those of the Severn region for at least a century longer. Villas in northern France, Belgium, and the Rhinelands were similarly affected a few decades later, although here too, as late as the mid-sixth century, a few clung to a precarious existence in the Moselle valley. In Bavaria, near the upper Danube, villas also began to disappear about the year 500, with only a few in remote Alpine valleys lingering on. As for the middle and lower Danube region, our scant evidence suggests that here too, as well as in the interior of the Balkan Peninsula, few villas survived later than the reign of Justinian. In this part of Europe, by the year 565, the Roman villa, like the Roman town, had become a thing of the past.

Quite different, however, was the fate of towns and villas further from the frontiers, except in such areas as northwestern Spain and Gascony, where conditions came to approximate those found in Britain or Bavaria. In most of Spain, in Italy, in central and southern Gaul, and in coastal regions of the Balkans, towns did not owe their existence to Imperial administration or to military demand. Therefore, the collapse of the Empire affected them very little; it may even in some cases have helped them, by relieving them of the taxes that had been levied by the late Roman government. This helps to explain the prosperity of Theodoric's Italy, and the reason why there was resistance to Justinian's tax-gatherers, who followed in the wake of his conquering armies.

In these same parts of Europe, villas also continued to exist, in contrast to their disappearance elsewhere. In part, this was because barbarian rulers of the Visigoths, Ostrogoths, Burgundians, and Franks were willing to use force, as the Roman government had done, to protect villa proprietors, members of the old Roman senatorial aristocracy, in return for the latter's continued assistance to their governments, in which they served as administrators. The apparent eagerness with which

members of the old Roman senatorial class, such as
Cassiodorus, Avitus, or Sidonius, served such rulers
could not have been unconnected with the desire to
secure protection for their estates. Even Justinian, once
Italy had been reconquered, shows in his legal enactments (called *Novellae*) a desire to strengthen the
villa system of the peninsula after his long campaign
there. By 565, villas, like towns, had managed to survive in much of what had once been Roman Europe.
(See Map 1.)

MONEY ECONOMIES

Finally, evidence seems to show that the use of a
money economy followed much the same pattern as that
revealed by our analysis of villa and town survival. The
barbarian kings of Spain and Italy continued to issue
gold and silver coins, which bore the names of Roman
emperors and were similar in weight and value to those
used in the Eastern Roman world. When Justinian
reconquered much of the barbarian West he continued
this coinage for the lands he regained.

In Gaul, initially, a somewhat different situation prevailed. Here gold coins were no longer being minted by
the late fifth century; the tendency was to replace them
in certain areas by local silver coins, or by bronze money
of little value, called *minimissimi*. Once the Franks
had won most of Gaul, however, a gold coinage reap-
peared, similar to that used in Italy and Spain and
bearing the name of the emperor in Constantinople.
By 565 most of Gaul, to judge from the money it used,
was again part of a Mediterranean region that used a
common gold currency.

Britain during this period presents a different picture
from Gaul. Here gold and silver coins seem to have

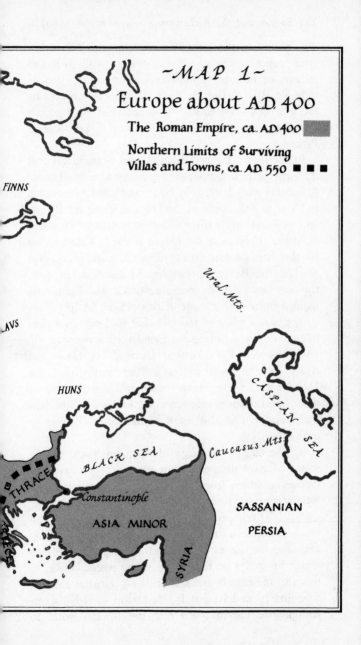

~MAP 1~
Europe about A.D. 400

The Roman Empire, ca. A.D. 400

Northern Limits of Surviving
Villas and Towns, ca. A.D. 550 ■ ■ ■

FINNS

SLAVS

HUNS

Ural Mts.

CASPIAN SEA

THRACE

BLACK SEA

Caucasus Mts.

Constantinople

ASIA MINOR

SYRIA

GREECE

SASSANIAN
PERSIA

disappeared by the early fifth century, with only a few crude copper coins which numismatists call barbarous *radiates* or bronze minimissimi continuing to circulate near old Roman forts in Kent and Gloucestershire. By the year 565 even these had disappeared, as a money economy ceased to have any meaning in post-Roman Britain.

In Germany, Central Europe, and Scandinavia still a fourth pattern developed, especially at first. Thanks to contact with Italy, gold coins continued to circulate in German areas south of the Danube, along the Rhine, and in Frisia, while silver money was used as far north as Mainz. Even more interesting is the fact that, down to the end of Justinian's reign, Roman gold coins reached the Baltic in considerable numbers. In part, this was because trade routes across Central Europe remained open during most of this period. Mainly however, it was a result of the fact that gold subsidies paid to the Huns and Ostrogoths found their way north. By 565, however, the situation changed, as Slavs and Avars cut the trade routes leading north from the Danube. Scandinavia then ceased to enjoy the use of money and relapsed into economic localism, a situation that came to prevail in most of the lower Danube region as well.

By the end of the reign of Justinian, then, money seems to have disappeared in most of those parts of Europe in which towns and villas had ceased to exist, leaving much of Roman Europe, like barbarian Europe, with a relatively primitive economy. All of Britain, and much of northern France, Belgium, and Germany, along with the interior of the Balkans, now found its economic life based on the village or the pastoral tribe, as was also the case in Ireland, Scotland, Central Europe, Scandinavia, and Russia. It was almost as if barbarian Europe had moved south into the Roman world to

wipe out over large areas the urbanization, industrializa-
tion, villa system, and monetary exchanges that were
typical of the more advanced economic world that
still existed to the south. Not everything was destroyed
in the process, however. Near old Roman production
centers in Britain, and along the Rhine and Danube,
traditions of skill and craftsmanship remained, as the
Sutton Hoo treasure and the researches of the distinguished French archeologist Edouard Salin have
proven. These were to blossom again when conditions
proved more propitious.

In the part of Europe that lay closer to the Mediterranean, however, things were quite different. Here contact was maintained with the prosperous world of the
eastern Mediterranean; it even increased in importance
as Vandal piracy subsided. Trade was largely in the
hands of Jewish, Syrian, and Greek merchants, who
exchanged such Eastern luxury products as wine,
papyrus, spices, and silks for Western products, and
especially slaves. Justinian's reconquest of much of the
West further stimulated commerce here.

In emphasizing the economic continuity of this part
of Europe with its Roman past, however, it would be
unwise to exaggerate, as Pirenne did, the importance
of the Eastern merchants located in western Europe, or
to overstate the value of the trade they carried on.
It is significant that Merovingian Gaul used no silver
coins in the early sixth century. This suggests that its
trade with the East affected its upper classes and not the
mass of the population—unless, as is possible, they relied on trade goods rather than money as the basis of
their exchanges. And we need to note that much of
Merovingian gold came not as a result of trade, but
from booty and Byzantine subsidies, which allowed
Frankish society to purchase luxury products it could
not otherwise have afforded.

Social Relations and Interrelations

PERSISTENCE AND CHANGE

In those parts of Europe that remained subject to control by the Eastern Roman emperors, or which were reconquered by Justinian, few basic social changes took place. Society continued to be composed of a mass of servile coloni and a class of large landowners who belonged to the senatorial aristocracy, in addition to a small middle class of merchants who lived in the surviving towns, and were numerous only in such a metropolis as Constantinople. Justinian may have lessened the political power of the landed aristocracy within the Empire, but he did not interfere with their social or economic status as privileged citizens.

Beyond the boundaries of the Empire, however, in regions that had once been Roman, but were now ruled by barbarian kings, a special problem existed. This had to do with the relationship between the Roman and the German, or barbarian, elements in the population. Judging from later law codes, it seems that the solution initially attempted was to separate these two groups. Each was made subject to different laws, and intermarriage was forbidden. Since most invading Germans were Arians, religious differences sharpened the legal and social differentiation that was attempted.

This legal and religious separation was matched by a functional one, between German and Roman upper classes. In Spain, Italy, and much of Gaul, an aristocracy of Roman descent continued to run such civil government as survived from Roman times, and to monopolize high church offices. The Germans, on the other hand, provided the armed forces for these kingdoms, just as they had done during the last years of the Roman Empire in the West. In practice, this pattern was also followed in much of the Eastern Roman Empire, where Germans—especially the Ostrogoths—provided Constantinople with its most dependable troops during the fifth century, and where Belisarius and Narses recruited their armies from the ranks of outside barbarian peoples. What was new in parts of the West was the legal distinction between these two groups.

Considerable legal activity was required in western Europe to maintain this distinction between German and Roman. Although a special mid-fifth century Theodosian Code, compiled in Constantinople, had spread throughout the West, where it remained in force for the Roman population, German rulers were not content with this alone. They therefore issued additional law codes for their Roman subjects, and began to reduce to written form their own customary law, which had applied to their own peoples. Thus, by the early sixth century, we find the law of the Salian Franks first written down and the *Lex Visigothorum* (Law of the Visigoths) and the *Lex Burgundiorum* (Law of the Burgundians) taking form. These barbarian codes, with their emphasis upon law as a method of stopping private blood feuds among kindred groups, and their elaborate systems of fines and proof by ordeal, represented legal attitudes very different from those that were found in Roman law. Even more important, their appearance marks a basic change in how law was conceived in much of Europe. Now law became a personal affair, rather than a territorial one, and the law a man followed depended not on the region in which he lived, but on the group to which he belonged. Personality of the law had become the rule beyond the borders of the Roman Empire ruled from Constantinople.

FREEDOM AND DEPENDENCE

In the barbarian parts of Europe, beyond the relatively civilized area, we find a somewhat different social pattern. This was village Europe, rather than villa Europe, and few large estates existed. Here lived a relatively large class of free alodial landowners, who were the fighting men of the period. This society was once thought of as essentially democratic. It was, in fact, a good deal more aristocratic than it seems at first glance. In practice, a small group of kings, chiefs, nobles, and freemen dominated a larger body of clients and thralls, or conquered natives. Many of the former had actually much in common with the surviving Roman aristocracy, who were serving barbarian kings in much of western Europe. Thus, despite laws prohibiting it, we soon find intermarriage taking place between these two groups, and the beginning of a single class of noble landowners, who were to dominate most of the continent during the early Middle Ages.

As privileged landowners, from the rulers on downward, came to dominate less privileged coloni and clients, by the mid-sixth century we already find a proto-feudal or proto-seigneurial system coming into existence. It is useless to argue whether this system was basically German or Roman. It had obvious roots both in the German war-band, as described by Tacitus, which had been continued in the bodyguards of German chiefs and kings, and in certain dependent relationships, known as the *patronicum, beneficium,* and *precarium,* during the Late Empire. In these lawless times, the weak were forced to seek the assistance of the strong, who furnished them with protection and sustinence, in return for service that was often of a military nature. A lord-vassal relationship thus began to develop everywhere from royal court to countryside estate. This was true even in Byzantium, where the large force of fighting men that Belisarius raised from his own estates to protect Constantinople shows the same sort of system emerging that we find among the Franks and the Visigoths.

In practice, as well as in theory, such personal relationships had not yet come to provide the basis for the armed forces of this period. German kings still depended upon armed freemen to provide them with the troops they needed, and Roman emperors still used hired mercenaries. These things were beginning to change, however, as large landowners began to muster those private armies that were much later to form the basis of Europe's feudal system.

The Church

Just as other aspects of life were changed during this period, so was its most important institution, the Christian Church. By the year 400, the Orthodox Church within the Empire had become a state Church, and all rival religions had been banned. A long struggle between Arians and Trinitarians had ended in a victory for the latter, and the Arians had been driven out of the Empire as heretics. This new state Church had developed a well-organized hierarchy, and its special privileges had been recognized by the Imperial government. It had shown that even as powerful an emperor as Theodosius was subject to its moral laws. During this same century, the new force of monasticism, which had originated in Egypt, had spread rapidly throughout the Eastern Empire, although it had, as yet, made little impression upon the Latin West. The Church in 400 was still a united one, despite St. Jerome's Latin translation of the Bible, which had begun to emphasize certain differences between the East and the West.

CAESAROPAPISM IN THE EAST

The fifth century affected the Latin Church and the Greek Church quite differently. The Church in Constantinople and in the part of Europe that was ruled by Eastern emperors had to face two special problems, heresy and Caesaropapism. The problem of heresy arose as a result of doctrinal differences concerning the nature of Christ. First Nestorianism overemphasized Jesus' human nature, and was declared heretical by the Council of Ephesus in 431. Then Monophysitism overemphasized Jesus' divine nature, and was in its turn condemned by the Council of Chalcedon in 451. Nestorianism proved comparatively easy to suppress, and its adherents were driven from the Empire. Monophysitism, however, proved more difficult to handle, since Syria, Egypt, and Armenia refused to accept the verdict of Chalcedon, although this decision was acclaimed in the more Greek parts of the Eastern Roman world. When persecution proved ineffective, such emperors as Zeno and Anastasius attempted compromise, ignoring Chalcedon and defying the wishes of Constantinople and the Greek areas in an attempt to hold their Empire together.

At the same time, fifth-century emperors in the East emphasized their role as heads of the Church, a tradition they had inherited from Constantine. They did not hesitate to remove from office those churchmen with whose policies and views they disagreed. Since they felt it necessary to conciliate Monophysite Syria and Egypt, they were especially concerned with controlling the Church, lest controversy split their Empire apart. Thus they laid the foundations of the Caesaropapism that, in later centuries, was often to distinguish the Greek Church from the Latin Church in the West.

INDEPENDENCE OF THE HIERARCHY IN THE WEST

In the West, special circumstances had increased the prestige of the Papacy and of those bishops and archbishops that headed the Church hierarchy. In the first place, since neither Nestorianism nor Monophysitism had any Western adherents, the Latin Church led by the Pope could throw its full strength against these heresies at the Church councils that were convened to deal with them. This tipped the scales against both, and gained prestige for the Papacy as the guardian of Orthodoxy throughout the entire Christian world. On a more practical level, since Western emperors were weak in the fifth century and had transferred their capital from Rome to Ravenna, the Popes were left without any immediate secular authorities strong enough to restrain them. The resulting independence that they enjoyed allowed them to negotiate with barbarian invaders on their own initiative, as Pope Leo did with Attila the Hun in 452, and thus to gain further prestige for themselves.

Still another factor that increased the independence and prestige of the Church hierarchy in the West was the Arianism that most of the German invaders professed. This caused the mass of the orthodox Roman population, as the Empire collapsed, to look to their own bishops as their natural protectors against heretical rulers and invaders—a situation that could result in real authority for such churchmen. In Gaul, for instance, when Clovis abandoned paganism for Christian Orthodoxy in the late fifth century, he immediately rallied to his side the entire Church and most of the Gallo-Roman population; this facilitated his victories over the Arian Visigoths and the pagan Alemanni. Similarly, Justinian's reconquests in the West were aided by the fact that he came as a champion of Orthodoxy against heretical German rulers. For, as the Roman Empire came to its end in the West, more and more it was the Church and its orthodox bishops in whose hands lay much of whatever leadership and public authority survived.

There was more to it than this, however. One of the chief functions of the Roman senatorial class during the Late Empire had been to serve the Empire as bureaucrats and administrators—a role they continued to play for barbarian kings. But as time passed, more and more of them began to desert service in the state for Church careers. Thus Sidonius Appolinaris, who served mid-century Western emperors as a high official, ended his life, not as a bureaucrat but as a bishop, defending the Gallo-Roman population of his part of Gaul from barbarian attack. Cassiodorus, who served as Theodoric's chief minister for a period, finally deserted secular affairs to end his career in the monastery of Vivarium. St. Benedict, whose family were of the local Roman nobility, turned his back on government service to find his destiny in the monastery of Monte Cassino. The Church was now increasingly attracting the kind of able administrators that earlier had served Roman emperors and their German successor kings.

MONASTICISM

One other aspect of the Church during this period needs to be discussed—monasticism. In the East, monasticism continued to develop along the lines laid down by St. Basil in the fourth century. In the West, it followed different paths, one of the more interesting being the form it developed in Celtic Britain and Ireland. Here Christianity itself took firm root during the fourth century, though it seems probable that most of the British population became Christian only after the withdrawal of Roman troops in the early fifth century. As this happened, the vital form that Church organization took was monastic—best seen, perhaps, at St. Ninian's monastery, which was known as the White House. It was in this form that British Christianity spread to Ireland, whose conversion is traditionally associated with the work of St. Patrick. By the middle of the sixth century, a distinctive Irish Christian organization had emerged, which had been grafted onto Ireland's tribal system.

This organization was based on abbeys ruled by lord abbots, who were more important than bishops, and who exercised a large measure of control over the lay population that lived near such establishments. Irish monks wore a different tonsure from that of other Western monks, and celebrated Easter on a different date. Their emphasis and their practices were strongly ascetic. What really most distinguished them, however, was the fact that they recognized no hierarchical control over them. Although they tended to be quarrelsome as well as independent-minded, they put great store in learning, and established schools in their monasteries that soon attracted large numbers of students, who were instructed in Greek as well as in Latin. By 565, they were also beginning to emerge as an active missionary force in Europe.

On the continent, other forms of Western monasticism also developed during these years. Of these, the most popular type, seen in such centers as Lerins in southern France, tended to be anti-intellectual and to emphasize a retreat from the world much like that found in Egypt and other Oriental regions. Then this began to change, thanks to St. Benedict. Having decided to desert the world and find solace in religion, Benedict lived first as a hermit in the mountains just south of Rome. Convinced that such an anchorite existence left much to be desired, he abandoned it to found a monastery at Monte Cassino, where he became the first abbot. There, in the early sixth century, he established what we know as the Rule of St. Benedict. As modified a little later by Pope Gregory the Great, it became the basis of Latin monastic organization. It had a number of salient characteristics: it stressed moderation, order, and discipline; it set up a division of labor among the monks, so that the abbey could be economically self-sufficient; thirdly, by providing a library and study for the monks, it made it possible for a monastery to serve as a center of learning. Although it was not until after Benedict's death that his rule began to spread throughout western Europe, Monte Cassino did serve as a model of what an effectively organized Latin monasticism could be like.

It must be emphasized, however, that by 565 only the very first steps had been taken toward the development of a distinctive European Latin Christendom. For instance, papal prestige, so real during the fifth century, suffered an eclipse when Justinian, after his conquest of Italy, turned theologian and quarreled with the Pope, who refused to accept his doctrinal innovations. This led to the Pope's forcible removal into exile and a consequent loss of papal prestige. Except in Gaul, most Germans in the West remained Arians and separate from the mass of the population. In such areas as Anglo-Saxon Britain, northwestern

Spain, and most of Germany, as well as in the country-side generally, paganism was the rule; only Ireland, beyond Rome's old frontiers, accepted Christianity. Except for certain Celtic areas, monasticism still remained on the whole uninterested in learning. The elements that were to make for a vital, expanding western European Church were present, but they had not yet become fused, so as to form a new and special leadership for Europe.

Cultural Life

When we turn from an examination of the Church to the general culture of the period, we find ourselves forced to recognize, to begin with, that a variety of cultural levels and accomplishments existed in various parts of Europe. Indeed, we can divide the continent into four distinct cultural areas.

LAW AND LETTERS

The level of civilization in the part of Europe that had remained Roman continued to be remarkably high. A large class of educated laymen remained in existence in Constantinople, and the essential elements of an educational system that had been inherited from the late Roman world continued unchanged. Although Justinian closed Athens' schools of pagan philosophy, classical and Christian authors went on being studied in well-organized municipal and private schools. Of particular importance was the study of Roman law. It was in Constantinople that the Theodosian Code was issued in the middle of the fifth century; it was there, some eighty years later, that the even more important

Justinian Code was compiled by learned jurists. This latter code, whose influence spread west into parts of Italy and Spain, summed up for all time the legal traditions of Rome at their best.

Almost as important is the evidence of a literary renaissance during the early sixth century, especially in the writing of history. The ornament of this revival was Procopius, whose *History of the Wars* of Justinian, written in Greek, was the best historical narrative composed since the time of Ammianus Marcellinus in the fourth century. To it Procopius added other works such as *On Buildings* and *Anecdota*, which gave us additional information about his era. In a legal and literary sense, then, one can see no evidence of a decline in the culture of that part of Europe that had remained Roman.

In a second region, however, more changes took place. Something of the late Roman secular tradition of rhetoric survived in parts of the civilized West, as we learn from the poems and letters of Sidonius. A little while later, a definite intellectual and literary revival took place in Ravenna, at the court of Theodoric. Here Cassiodorus showed a continuing interest in rhetoric, while his fellow Roman scholar, Boethius, provides us with an example of an author who was still concerned with neoplatonic philosophical ideas. It was the latter's plan to translate the entire corpus of the works of Plato and Aristotle into Latin, a task he was unfortunately only able to begin. His *Consolation of Philosophy*, written as he awaited death in Theodoric's prison, shows some grasp of classical philosophical ideas and their presentation in a somewhat original form. Nor was Theodoric's court circle concerned only with rhetoric and philosophy. It was interested in history, too, for Cassiodorus composed a long history of the Goths, which is now lost and is available to us only in the abridged form that we know as Jordanes' *Gaetica*.

This intellectual activity at Ravenna unfortunately did not survive Justinian's reconquest of Italy. Boethius had no successors, and Cassiodorus, who had retired to his monastery after the fall of the Ostrogoths, had no influence upon the next generation of Italians. Similarly in Gaul and in Spain, we find no one following in Sidonius' footsteps or sharing his cultural interests. Secular literary culture in this part of Europe lacked the depth and vitality it was still able to exhibit in Constantinople.

An interest in law, however, seems to have been more real. We not only have Theodoric's Edict, but the *Lex Romanorum* of the Burgundians and the Breviary of Alaric as well, to show how German kings continued to codify Roman law for their Roman subjects. If Justinian's Code had little impact beyond Italy, this was in no small measure due to the fact that it was not needed in the West, which was still producing its own distinctive codes of Roman law.

CHRISTIAN LITERATURE IN THE WEST

It is in the field of Christian as opposed to secular culture, however, that the West shows the most evidence of vitality. And here it is the early fifth-century figure of St. Augustine, with his view of belief as superior to knowledge, who had the most influence. His writings, which set the intellectual tone of the next six centuries in the West, were much admired, particularly his *City of God*; along with Orosius' *Seven Books of History Against the Pagans*, it provided a Christian rationale that explained the fall of the Western Empire and separated the Church from its too close embrace by the secular state. Almost as important in emphasizing a special Christian point of view were Salvian's *De Gubernaterione Dei* and the works of Caesarius of Arles. As the Empire declined and the educated upper classes were increasingly attracted to the Church, their intellectual interests became Christian too. These interests help to explain the numerous "Saints' Lives" that began to appear and were immensely popular; for these "Christian romances," as they have been called, fitted the mood and the needs of the period.

INTELLECTUAL ACTIVITY OUTSIDE
THE ROMAN WORLD

One finds much less evidence of intellectual activity in former Roman territory in Britain, northern Gaul, and Germany. Here was produced the Law of the Salian Franks, which attempts to provide a written code for a barbarian people, to match those legal codes that the Roman population possessed. And we find that disappointing work that Gildas produced in sub-Roman Britain, in a barbarous Latin. That is all. Yet here also "Saints' Lives" were being composed, of which the most important were *The Life of St. Patrick* and *The Life of St. Germanus*. It was from the former that the many Irish and British "Saints' Lives" of the next few centuries were to be derived, while the latter provided a popular model for later Merovingian hagiography.

Beyond what had been the Roman world, however, we have little evidence of any written tradition whatsoever, except that provided by Scandinavian runic writing, whose peculiar orthography is found carved on stones in various parts of the Scandinavian world, and by a number of examples of the writing that decorates those carved monuments known as Ogham stones, scattered throughout Celtic Britain and Ireland. To be sure, there was an oral poetic tradition in existence, which was to be later reflected in such works as *Beowulf*, the legends of Ermaneric and Dietrich, and the Norse Eddas and Irish legends. And no doubt bards were already singing their tales of heroic valor in the halls of Celtic and German chieftains and barbarian kings, but we have no contemporary evidence to prove this. Beyond the Rhine, Danube, and Britain, barbarian Europe remained untouched by the culture that survived in the rest of the continent.

ART AND ARCHITECTURE

When we turn to art and architecture, we find an equally interesting pattern. Although we find some description in *Beowulf* of what a German chieftain's great hall was like, none of the wooden architecture that prevailed beyond Rome's old frontiers has come down to us. A few surviving examples of building techniques in Britain, such as Caerleon's fifth-century walls, show a decline in the art of fortification, while remains of Saxon dwellings outside the walls of Roman Canterbury reveal the simple style of construction that was all that the barbarians of the early sixth century could manage.

In at least two other areas of the continent, however, we find more interesting architectural developments. Procopius' volume *On Buildings* tells us of Justinian's extensive building program, which included fortresses, public buildings, and churches. The most remarkable of these was his great church of Hagia

Sophia in Constantinople, where his architects surpassed their earlier Roman predecessors in inventiveness by solving the problem of how to cover a huge square area with a round dome. The success of their plan helped to inaugurate the great Byzantine style of later centuries.

Architecture in Italy, especially at Rome and Ravenna, developed significant features too. By studying Roman churches built during this period, we can see how the basilican church developed out of earlier Roman forms, to set the pattern for later church buildings of this type in western Europe. Ravenna provides a series of architectural gems, which begins with the fifth-century tomb of Galla Placidia, continues with churches and baptisteries built in Theodoric's time, and ends with churches built by Justinian. The result is a group of buildings that stand as a living museum of the architectural styles that developed over a century.

Art during these years seems even more interesting than architecture, and we possess many examples of it. In the Eastern Roman world, in Italy, and in parts of Gaul, we find evidences of a continuing classical tradition of sculpture, especially when we examine sarcophagi, ivories, and the like. We find similar classical elements in the mosaic art of the time. At both Rome and Ravenna, however, we find these classical themes beginning to change and develop into a new style, which reaches its apogee in the magnificent portraits of Justinian and Theodora in the Church of San Vitale in Ravenna. These reveal the new flatness, the transcendental tendency and the brilliance of color that are to distinguish the Byzantine style from that which had gone before.

Side by side with this classical artistic style, some of which was becoming Byzantine in character, was another major artistic trend—an essentially nonclassical, barbarian one. It seems to have had its origin mainly in the Iranian-Scythian art of Central Asia which, even before the fall of the Western Empire, had reached Russia and Scandinavia. During the fifth century its influence increased, as it became the dominant mode of artistic expression of the Germanic peoples and, in the form of a decoration employed on metal objects and known as *barbaricini*, began to affect metal work in Roman Gaul. German invaders carried this style with them into Britain, Spain, and Italy as well. Its best expression during these years is found in magnificent gold jewelry that has been unearthed in Scandinavia, in belt buckles that Salin has found in graves in Frankish Gaul, in Anglo-Saxon jewelry from Kent and East Anglia, or in Hunnic gems from sites in Central Europe.

Finally, we have evidence of a fourth form of artistic expression, the Celtic. Although we find evidence of the existence of this style in Roman Britain in the fourth century, it was only after the end of the Roman occupation that it began to be diffused over a wide area. We can see it revealed in the Ogham stones we have mentioned, and in copper and bronze kettles that have been discovered in many areas of the British Isles, as well as in the so-called tomb of Merobaudes at Poitiers. More related in some ways to Coptic, Syrian, and Armenian art than to that of the late Roman world, it had already begun to exert an influence on northwestern Europe.

Summary

As the Western Roman Empire disappeared, then, what we find in much of Europe is both continuity and change. Continuity seems most evident in those heavily Romanized parts of Europe that not only kept the villa system and the town alive, but also maintained intellectual and artistic traditions derived from the immediate late Roman past. At the same time, in both the Roman East and in Italy, classical artistic elements were being transmuted into something new—the Byzantine style of the future, while among the German and Slavic peoples of barbarian Europe a very different style, derived from Central Asia, spread south into the former Roman world. This and an equally unique Celtic art were to remain important in later centuries, as Europe moved toward a very different destiny.

✑§ chapter II §✑

Monks and Warriors,

A.D. 565-718

T he years that separate the death of Justinian in 565 from the second great Arab attack on Constantinople in 717–718 saw changes in Europe as important as those that attended the barbarian invasions. Yet in some ways, down to the very end of the period, these changes seem less important in the political sphere than in any other. In 565 Europe was dominated by four powers: the Roman Empire, the Kingdom of the Franks, the Kingdom of the Visigoths, and the Avars. This continued to be true until the early eighth century, although we might add to the list a strong Lombard kingdom in northern Italy. Nevertheless, a new political element was being added to Europe as consolidation proceeded beyond the regions dominated by these states. This was to be seen in the rise of a series of Anglo-Saxon kingdoms in the British Isles. It also led to first steps toward political consolidation in Scandinavia. It explains the appearance of the first Slavic kingdom in Central Europe, that of Samo. And it is to this impulse that we owe the emergence of a new Bulgaria in the Balkans and of a Kazar kingdom in south Russia. What had been a formless barbarian Europe in 565, by 718 had begun to take on political substance.

One might well ask what this new element was. It consisted essentially of a political organization under hereditary kings, which tended to extend itself over relatively large areas and in so doing subordinated pre-existing tribal, clan, and kinship groups. Everywhere it appeared, this new political element endowed kings with a certain overall judicial, military, and administrative authority, which they tended to exercise through a rudimentary household organization, or by means of a large war-band of followers located at their court, or through a Church hierarchy or pagan priesthood that was increasingly under their control. In short, the level of political consolidation in certain areas of Europe was, during this period, beginning to reach the level achieved in parts of central Africa, such as Uganda, at the time when these regions were discovered by European explorers in the mid-nineteenth century.

Meanwhile, to the southeast of Europe there arose, within a few short decades, the new and mighty empire of Islam. Ten years after the death of its founder, Mohammed, it had wrested Syria, Egypt, and Libya from the Roman Empire. By the year 711, it had added the rest of North Africa to its dominion and spilled over into Europe to overwhelm Visigothic Spain. After a relatively quiet century and a half, Europe, accustomed to a seemingly eternal Romania to the south and east of it, awoke to find itself faced by a very different and powerful Islamic world. The year 718 marked the end of one era and the beginning of

another, which was to see a change in all of Europe's
internal and external relationships.

The Great Powers

THE ROMAN EMPIRE

Down to the time of the Islamic conquest of Spain,
the most important power in Europe remained the
Roman Empire. In 565 it included within its actual
boundaries southern Spain, the islands of the Mediterranean, Italy, and most of the Balkans south of the
Danube, and it influenced the rest of civilized and
barbarian Europe through the use of subsidies in gold
and a cautious, wise diplomacy. Although some territory in Italy was lost to the Lombards after Justinian's
death, and Slavs infiltrated the Balkans as far south
as the Peloponnesus, when Maurice died in 602, the
power of the Roman Empire was still unrivaled. It
controlled the Mediterranean with its fleet, and continued to hold most of the important centers in Italy
and along the coasts of the Balkans.

Early in the seventh century, things began to change.
Invasions by the Persians, followed by Arab attacks at
the end of the reign of Heraclius, threatened the Empire with dissolution. Heraclius rallied his forces to
defeat the Persians, but Islam's conquest of Syria and
Egypt proved to be permanent, and was followed a
half century later by the loss of North Africa. During
this period, the Empire's territory in Europe was also
affected. The Visigoths recovered Andalusia; the Lombards took Genoa; and the Empire's territory in the
Balkans shrank, under Avar and Slavic pressure, until
it included only a few coastal regions.

Nevertheless, as late as the last years of the seventh

century, Byzantium's power in Europe still remained formidable. Despite Arab assaults on Constantinople, its navy continued to rule the Mediterranean and control its islands. It held Rome, Ravenna, Venice, and Naples, and its emperor, Constans II, could appear in Italy as late as the mid-seventh century with a large army, and carry into captivity a Pope with whom he disagreed. The Empire's subsidies and diplomacy continued to play an important role in European politics, while its merchants dominated much of Europe's external commerce.

Even the change in the Empire's governmental and military system, which took place under the shock of Persian and Arab assaults, did not necessarily weaken Byzantium. This change saw military and civil administration in the provinces combined to form governing units called *themes*, which could be defended by a local citizen militia instead of by hired mercenary soldiers—thus expanding a system inaugurated by Justinian and Maurice for Italy into one that was applicable to the entire Empire. Yet this may have made the Empire even stronger, since citizen soldiers who were defending their homes had more incentive to fight than did hired levies. In short, by the eighth century, despite loss of territory, this Empire was still militarily and navally strong in Europe, and destined to remain so.

THE KINGDOMS OF THE FRANKS AND THE VISIGOTHS

The second most powerful European state was the kingdom of the Franks, at least down to the end of the reign of Dagobert, who was a contemporary of Heraclius. The Frankish kingdom, which was divided periodically among quarrelling Merovingians, had the advantage of a large warrior class and of roots in Germany that allowed its military manpower to be easily replenished. For more than a century after the reign of Clovis, its kings, who ruled as autocrats, were able to maintain a relatively effective government, although on a basis more rudimentary than that of Byzantium. They controlled a subservient church and were relatively well supplied with money.

After Dagobert, things worsened, as short-lived kings constantly subdivided their kingdoms, thus helping localism to triumph over royal centralism. Gradually, the Merovingians lost control over outlying parts of their realm, while their nuclear kingdoms of Neustria and Austrasia, once the nobility was out of control, fell into the hands of "mayors of the palace." By the time a Carolingian family had united Austrasia and Neustria in 718, most of the Frankish kingdom was no longer controlled by the central authorities.

The kingdom of the Visigoths, which came to include the entire Iberian Peninsula and part of southern France during these years, matched that of the Franks in importance, although it had been weaker earlier. Soon after its ruling class abandoned Arianism for Orthodoxy, at about the time of Gregory the Great, its kings expelled the Byzantines from Andalusia; at the same time, they maintained their hold on Septimania, despite Frankish attacks, and called together great national Church councils, which increased royal authority. Nevertheless, as the seventh century drew to a close, Visigothic kings, like their Merovingian contemporaries, found their church and nobility increasingly difficult to control, while their persecution of the Jews, who lived in the cities, caused these latter to become disaffected. Few Visigothic monarchs, all of whom were elected by important secular and ecclesiastical landholders whom we may call the magnates, were fortunate enough to die in bed. Equally important is the fact that the Arab conquest of the Near East began to dislocate trade, which cut royal revenues as Spain's prosperity declined. Even so, almost down to the time of the Moorish conquest of 711, Visigothic Spain remained a powerful state, one that seemed more likely to survive than that of the Merovingian Franks on the other side of the Pyrenees.

THE LOMBARDS

The third important kingdom in the West was that of the Lombards, which, like the Visigothic realm, developed strength only during the course of the seventh century. In the late sixth century, the Lombards were already powerful enough to conquer much of Italy from Byzantium, yet their monarchs had little authority beyond the Po valley. After Constans II's efforts to reconquer all of Italy had ended in failure, this situation began to change; Lombard kings formed a more centralized state from their capital at Pavia, subjecting their dukes to the royal will and making an attempt to codify Lombard law. During this period, they abandoned Arianism for Orthodoxy, and the improvement of economic conditions within their realm gave them more revenues. Although the southern Lombard duchies of Spoleto and Benevento remained autonomous, by 718 the Lombard kingdom had begun to match those of the Franks and Visigoths in political importance.

AVARS, BULGARS, KAZARS

East of the Franks and the Lombards lay the other really important state of the period, that of the Avars.

It was composed of tribes of raiding nomads, whose control of the Hungarian plain was the basis of their power, but who also exercised authority over most of their Slavic neighbors, by incorporating them into their Empire and forcing them to fight in their armies. In the early seventh century, they were powerful enough to send an army to besiege Constantinople and at about the same time to threaten Dagobert's German domains. Avar strength, however, declined soon after this period, probably because their Slavic allies demanded more independence, and because the arrival of the Bulgars along the lower Danube restricted their power in that direction. By 718, even though they were still a threat to their neighbors, they could no longer dominate most of Central Europe.

As this Avar dominion passed its zenith, two new nomadic states began to arise in eastern Europe, that of the Bulgars and that of the Kazars. The Bulgars seem to have migrated from the steppes of south Russia and to have reached the lower Danube in the late seventh century. Despite campaigns waged against them by Justinian II, they were able to establish themselves in an area just north of the Rhodian Alps, from which they could easily threaten Constantinople. Like the Avars, they incorporated into their state a number of Slavic tribes who furnished them with additional manpower; like the Avars, they attacked Constantinople during the Arab assault of 717–718. By the early eighth century, they had begun to form a state that was to remain a problem for Byzantium for many centuries.

In some respects, the kingdom of the Kazars, which appeared in south Russia at about the same time, was even more important than that of the Bulgars. Its center of power lay just north of the Caucasus, between the Black Sea and the Caspian. From the start, the Kazars were allied to Byzantium, whom they supported in wars against the Moslems. They also drew strength from the fact that important trade routes passed through their territory: those linking the Black and Caspian seas with the Baltic, and another that reached China via the old Central Asian silk road. By 718 they had grown powerful enough to dominate southern Russia as far north as Kiev; by their halting of further nomadic advances west of Turkestan, they seem to have stabilized the political situation on these steppes for several centuries.

NEW POLITICAL ENTITIES IN THE NORTH

North of this relatively well-organized territory, which now stretched from the Atlantic to the Caspian, these years saw some political progress too. Perhaps the most significant of all the new political entities that appeared were those in Britain. Here the Anglo-Saxons, after driving the native Britons west into Cornwall, Wales, and Strathclyde, at last began to form political units that exhibited some cohesion. At the same time, first one and then another of these new kingdoms grew powerful enough to assume a certain political overlordship over the rest: first Kent, then East Anglia, then Northumbria, and finally Mercia. Nothing like a united Anglo-Saxon England emerged during these years, but we can see at least the basis for such a development.

Much more tentative were political groupings in Scandinavia and among the Slavs of Central Europe. As to Scandinavia, we hear of an Ivar Widefathom, who exercised authority over Sweden and other Baltic areas; a little while later, we learn of a first attempt to set up a Danish state. In Central Europe during these years, Samo created the first Slavic principality of which we have precise knowledge. It is doubtful whether any of these political entities were more than ephemeral creations, but they too point the way toward a more stable political future for these parts of Europe.

Between 565 and 718, there was thus a trend toward political consolidation, especially in those parts of Europe that had formerly been part of the Roman Empire. In the West we find relatively strong Visigothic, Frankish, and Lombard kingdoms, while in Britain new Anglo-Saxon states appear. To the east of these kingdoms and north of the Roman Empire three nomadic states arise—those of the Avars, Bulgars, and Kazars—which help stabilize the steppelands that stretch from Hungary to the Caspian. Beyond these areas, we also find tribal peoples in Scandinavia and Central Europe who were beginning to be affected by consolidation of a political sort. And it is worth noting that some of these states appeared, in whole or in part, beyond the old frontiers of the Roman Empire, which ceased to have any meaning for the Europe of this period. In the first years of the eighth century, however, this slow, orderly political development was suddenly affected by a new force, that of Islam, which spilled over into Europe to conquer Spain and to bring a new element into the European world. It is this new element that will engage our attention as we survey later centuries in the emergence of Europe.

Economic Developments

The economic developments of this period can best be understood if we divide them into two phases. One phase lasted for a little over a century, from the death of Justinian to the last days of Constantine IV (*ca.* 680). The second phase covered the next forty years, until the end of the second great Arab siege of Constantinople in 718. The first period was one of recovery from the disasters of the fifth century and of slow, steady economic growth in much of Europe. The second saw a crisis and serious dislocations, which changed economic life and laid the foundations of the very different Carolingian age that was to follow.

RECOVERY AND GROWTH

During the earlier period of growth, economic development owed something to political factors. Except in Italy, this was an age of relative peace and stability. In Visigothic Spain, in the kingdom of the Franks, in Anglo-Saxon England, in the realm of the Kazars, and even in Scandinavia this meant that commerce could be carried on without serious interruption, and that agriculture could develop with greater security than had hitherto been the case. Secondly, until well into the second half of the seventh century, Constantinople seems to have continued a policy of sending subsidies to her neighbors to further her diplomatic aims—which assured these peoples supplies of gold that might not otherwise have been available to them.

Thus Mediterranean trade reaching Spain, Gaul, and to some extent Italy, increased in importance during this century. Such commerce was still handled mainly by Eastern merchants—Syrians, Greeks, and Jews—who settled as far north as Paris, Trier, and Cologne, and who exchanged the Eastern wares they imported for gold, slaves, and Western products. In response to this trade, old Roman towns in northern Gaul, known as *civitates,* which had been moribund, again assumed an economic importance. Even as distant a city as Merida, in Spain, had a colony of Greek merchants within its walls. Some of this trade reached Britain, whose slaves and tin were much in demand in the Mediterranean, by way of a sea-route around Spain, or from Italy by way of the Rhine. The discovery of Coptic bronzes along routes linking Frisia and Italy and the fact that natron was used in Belgian glass proves such links with the Mediterranean. So also do the cowrie shells found in Kentish graves, which were probably used in trade as wampum was in colonial America, as well as objects from the world of Byzantium discovered at Sutton Hoo.

Important as was this revived international commerce, which again linked this part of northwestern Europe with the Mediterranean world, a more local traffic was probably even more vital. This commerce about the northern seas, from the Bay of Biscay to the Baltic, had all but disappeared in the preceding century. In the seventh century it began to revive, as western Gallic ports again traded with Spain, Ireland, and Britain and were joined by others along the Channel coast of France and in the Low Countries. As this commerce increased, it stimulated a revival of British trading-places, from Southampton to York. Nor did commerce stop here. Since Slavic and Avar advances had cut the central European trade routes that had led to the Baltic, Scandinavia's main contact with the more economically advanced south was now a maritime one, along the coasts of Frisia. Frisian and Anglo-Saxon traders became the main intermediaries along this route, carrying western European wares north in return for Baltic products.

Most of the goods exchanged along the trade routes that linked various areas of the northern seas were of natural origin: wine, foodstuffs, metals, and the like. Nevertheless, in parts of northern France, Belgium, the Rhinelands, and Britain, where late Roman industrial production had been heaviest, this age saw some revival of industry, with weapons, metalware, glass, pottery, and cloth mainly involved. Archeological finds in Scandinavia, dating from this period, show that some of these wares were already reaching the Hedeby region in southern Denmark and the Malar Sea area of Sweden in appreciable quantities.

A twofold economic growth, then, emerges from a study of the economic development of Europe during these years. One part of it was marked by an increase in commercial contacts between much of northern Europe and the Mediterranean world to the south. The second represented a revival of more local traffic about the northern seas of Europe, linking Ireland, Britain, and Scandinavia and the shores of Gaul and the Low Countries into a trading region of some importance. At the same time, this commerce, carried on by Irish, Anglo-Saxon, and Frisian traders, helped to revive moribund industries in northwestern Europe.

One aspect of this commercial revival was the gradual spread of the Mediterranean's gold coinage into parts of Europe where gold had been unknown for a century or more. (See Map 2.) This meant that northern French, Belgian, and Rhinelands civitates began to mint the larger gold coins, called *solidi*, and lighter ones, called *tremisses*, that had hitherto been restricted to Italy, Spain, and southern Gaul. Some were even minted in Britain and Frisia, although, judging from coin hoards, most gold pieces circulating there were of Frankish, Visigothic, or Byzantine origin. A similar situation prevailed in south Russia, where finds of Byzantium's gold coinage suggest an active economic and diplomatic contact with the Mediterranean world to the south.

This revival, however, had definite limitations. We have no evidence that gold coins of any sort circulated in Ireland, most of Britain, Scandinavia, Germany east of the Rhine and north of the Danube, or in northern and central Russia. Nor were there any mints in such regions. This suggests that the economic revival that spread north from the Mediterranean by the late seventh century did not manage to amalgamate the south with the trading region that was emerging about the northern seas. This came only much later.

CRISIS AND DISLOCATION

During the last years of the seventh century, even the limited economic revival came to an abrupt end. Syrian and Greek merchants suddenly disappeared from Gallic and Spanish civitates, leaving only a few Jews to carry on as an international merchant class in the West. Gold gradually disappeared, first from southern France, and then by 700 from Spain, Belgium, and the Rhinelands too. As this happened, a new, more local, silver coinage began to appear in Britain, and then spread throughout much of Europe north and west of Italy. This matches the situation in Russia, where a new silver dirhem coinage from Persia and the Moslem East spread north to the Baltic, along with objects of Eastern manufacture from the same parts of the world. Finally we find civitates disappearing in southern Gaul and much of Spain, as Anglo-Saxon merchants journeyed to Marseilles, and Frisians moved up the Rhine to procure Mediterranean wares that had earlier been available much further to the north. By the early eighth century, the only parts of Europe that still

MILES

0   100   200   300   400   500

NORTH SEA

BALTIC SEA

ICELAND

PICTS

SCOTS

ANGLES

BRITONS

SAXONS

FRISIANS

SAXONS

SLAVS

KINGDOM OF SAM

ATLANTIC OCEAN

NEUSTRIA

AUSTRASIA

FRANKISH KINGDOM

BASQUES

VISIGOTHIC KINGDOM

Toledo

LOM

Ravenna

SLAVS

BARDS

Rome

Naples

MEDITERRANEAN SEA

AFRICA

EASTERN ROMAN SEA

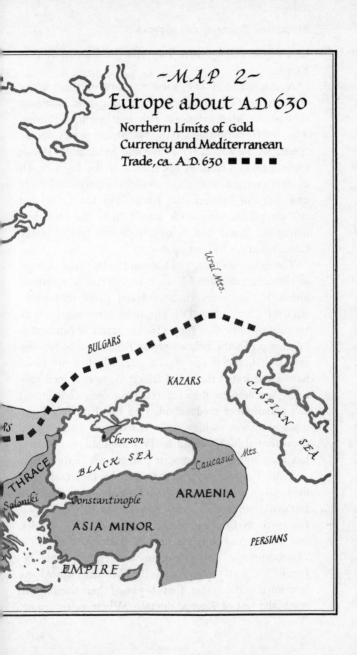

-MAP 2-
Europe about A.D. 630
Northern Limits of Gold
Currency and Mediterranean
Trade, ca. A.D. 630 ■ ■ ■ ■

Ural Mts.

BULGARS

KAZARS

CASPIAN SEA

RS

THRACE

Cherson

BLACK SEA

Caucasus Mts.

ARMENIA

Saloniki

Constantinople

ASIA MINOR

PERSIANS

EMPIRE

used a gold coinage were Italy and the Eastern Roman Empire.

As a result of all this, there was now only one active trade route that linked the Byzantine gold *nomismá* area of the Mediterranean with northwestern Europe. This led from northern Italy, via Alpine passes, to the North Sea by way of the Rhine and Moselle. Its Italian terminus was Venice at the mouth of the Po river. Its northern termini were those civitates in northern France and Belgium between the Rhine and the Loire that still carried on some trade with Britain and areas bordering the North Sea. A new trade axis typical of the Carolingian era had emerged.

The causes for these sudden and fundamental changes in the economic life of Europe are difficult to ascertain, although they seem to have taken place during the reign of Constantine IV. The most tempting explanation seems to be that they were the result of fundamental changes in the policies of the Roman, or as we now may call it, the Byzantine Empire, which alone could have inaugurated them and which alone remained relatively immune to their effects. One such change was the cessation of gold subsidies to the Empire's European neighbors—which explains why not a single gold coin minted by Constantine IV's immediate successors has been found in European coin hoards beyond Italy and the Empire itself. It may also be the result of a deliberate policy whereby Byzantium restricted her foreign commerce to a few specially chosen trade portals, such as Cherson in the Crimea, Venice, Naples, and Sicily. And it seems equally probable that, while Constantinople was willing to allow direct trade between her own empire and the Moslem world, she interfered with traffic that bypassed her territory to reach the rest of Europe directly. Whatever the cause, there can be little doubt that, by the early eighth century, a new pattern of commerce had arisen that was vitally to affect the future of Europe.

AGRICULTURE AND TECHNOLOGY

To fix our attention completely on commerce, merchants, industry, and the growth and decline of trading places, however, is to neglect an even more important aspect of European development, which took place in the countryside. In those parts of Europe where villas continued, there were no essential changes in the patterns of landholding or in methods of husbandry; these remained similar to the patterns found in late Roman times. In other parts of Europe, where the village was the unit of production, things began to change. Here, in areas of northern France, England, western Germany, and Slavic Europe, we find land now being cultivated that had earlier been either abandoned or neglected. Much of it was a heavy clay soil, which tended to be forested and was thus overlooked by the Romans and the barbarian peoples, since it was difficult to till. Now such land began to be cleared for cultivation in areas as different as the Loire valley, the forested slopes of Alsace, the bottom lands of Anglo-Saxon Britain, and the wooded flatlands of eastern Germany and Poland.

Some of this exploitation of new land resulted from peasant efforts to expand their fields as the population of their villages increased. Some of the land was cleared by monasteries that were established in areas where waste was plentiful. However it was broken to the plough, this new arable land was the cause for certain changes that affected rural society as a whole. Since such land tended to be more fertile than the light soils that the Romans and the earlier barbarian peoples had fa-

vored, the crops raised on it were more abundant.
Where it was used, then, food supplies increased and,
with them, population. Although only the first steps
were taken toward clearing waste and forest for agriculture in parts of northern Europe during these years, a
beginning was made that was to affect the future.

Since much of this new land was composed of wet,
low-lying clay soils, it encouraged the use of the heavy,
wheeled German plough rather than the light Mediterranean type. Such a plough could be used more effi-
ciently by employing horses for draft purposes, and
some have argued that this led to a borrowing from
the Avars of a horse collar and a set of rein attach-
ments that were totally new to the area. It is even
possible that, late in this period, the horseshoe was in-
vented in this part of Europe.

Technological innovations were not confined to
agriculture. They were matched by others that we find
in both western Europe and the East. One of the
more important was Greek fire, which originated in
China, was perfected in Byzantium, and made possible
successful resistance to enemy warships during the great
sieges of Constantinople of 626, 673–678, and 717–
718. Another innovation was the spread of the stirrup,
which began to revolutionize land warfare as much as
Greek fire had changed naval tactics, by making heavily
armed cavalry carrying lances the decisive battle-troops
of the period. We do not know exactly where the
stirrup originated, or when it began to spread throughout Europe. By the time of the Emperor Maurice, however, it was used by heavily armed Byzantine *ca-
taphracti*, or mounted warriors, and soon spread until
the Franks, the Visigoths, and other peoples in Central
Europe had adopted it. Where it was used, it revolutionized warfare by minimizing the importance of foot

soldiers and putting a premium on the mounted warrior, who tended to be drawn from the class of large landowners.

Other innovations in the Europe of this period seem to have been more local in origin. One was a new and superior type of pattern-welded sword that was made in the Rhinelands. Another consisted of better types of ships, which were being built in Ireland and the North Sea region, and which improved navigation. Finally, we have evidence of new weaving techniques, which helped develop the celebrated *pallia fresonica*, or Frisian cloth, of Carolingian times, just as silkworms, newly imported from China, helped lay the basis for a Byzantine silk industry of great future importance.

What emerges from all this is a view of the period between 565 and 718 that is quite different from that formerly held by many historians. This was not an age of economic stagnation in Europe, but of economic growth and the beginnings of technological change. Old trading places were revived, and new ones established, as commerce from the Mediterranean and about the northern seas increased in volume, despite the slowing down of this growth in the last decades of this period. Agriculture in parts of northern Europe began to develop greater productivity. An improved technology came forth with better ways of producing goods and transporting them, and even of waging war. A money economy began to spread into areas of Europe where for decades the use of money had been abandoned—first in the form of gold coins, then in the form of a more local silver currency. Though much remained to be done, by the early eighth century a new Europe was emerging, based on these changes; even a temporary decline could not long hinder it from reaching fruition.

Social Developments East and West

Changes in the social sphere were hardly less important. In western Europe, one of the more important was an end of the differentiation between the Roman and the barbarian element in the population. In the strictly legal sense, a distinction did survive, for each people clung to its individual law: Roman, Frankish, Visigothic, Lombard, or Anglo-Saxon. But in a practical sense, such distinctions ceased to have meaning, as an amalgamation of upper classes erased essential differences. Now, magnates of Roman background bore arms and were difficult to distinguish from the old German warrior class. Such an example as that of the Roman Arnulfings marrying German Pepinids to produce the Carolingians can be matched by numerous other such instances, drawn from the history of Visigothic Spain, Lombard Italy, or other parts of the Frankish domains. In Anglo-Saxon England, a Colin could become king of Wessex, while Northumbrian rulers welcomed alliances with their Celtic neighbors in Strathclyde. Everywhere distinctions that had seemed important earlier were becoming blurred. Nor was this confined to the higher levels of society. It occurred in every class, as the barriers that had separated Roman and barbarian ceased to have any real meaning.

There was, however, a growing gap that did separate an upper class of magnates, who controlled large estates, from a lower class of dependent cultivators or ordinary freemen. As noted earlier, this was nothing new in areas where the villa system of earlier Roman times survived. What was new was its extension into areas like the northern Frankish domains, or those parts of Lombard Italy where freeborn fighting men still existed. And it seems probable that this class distinction was accelerated by the spread of the stirrup, which put a premium on the mounted warrior and relegated the foot soldier to a less important role. Since only the large landowner in the West could afford to equip himself with the heavy war horse and expensive equipment that was now required for battle, it was this class that came to monopolize military power.

By the middle of the seventh century, the increasingly powerful magnate class had helped to weaken western European monarchs, whether they were Frankish, Visigothic, or Lombard, by making the monarchs dependent on their magnates, and thus lessening their control of their realms. At the same time, it gave these magnates effective control over the small proprietor class on the local level, since the latter could no longer depend on royal power for protection. As a result, proto-feudalism increased in importance. The resulting dependent personal relationships and the tenures that they encouraged, whether these were called *stipendia* in Visigothic Spain or *precaria* in France, or were those enjoyed by the *gasindi* of Lombard Italy, became a reality of the social structure of the time. Such tenures were, no doubt, slower to develop in Anglo-Saxon England and in those parts of Merovingian Germany where a freeborn warrior class still held its own. Even here, however, they were not unknown, especially along the Celtic borderlands, where we find a class of thanes appearing, or in Bavaria, close to the Avar frontier. In Scandinavia and Slavic Europe, such a development is unlikely to have occurred during this period. Nevertheless, in western Europe as a whole, we can see a great social change taking place, with an upper class of large landowners emerging as the elite fighting force of the period, and dominating their localities through dependent relationships and tenures that had to be accepted by the less fortunate members of society.

In Byzantium nothing of the sort took place, despite certain similar tendencies during the early sixth century. The main reason seems to be that emperors throughout this entire period had at their disposal supplies of money with which they could hire soldiers, something that Western monarchs did not possess. The armies that Maurice led across the Danube to fight the Avars, that Heraclius led against the Persians, and that Constans II brought to Italy—these were professional armies, paid in money. Thus, such rulers did not have to rely on their magnates, paid in land and privileges, to furnish them with troops that could be used in distant campaigns, as was the case in the West. The same is true of the small effective Imperial navy, stationed at Constantinople, that acquitted itself so well during the sieges of 626, 673–678, and 717–718.

When, during the course of the seventh century, mass attacks were launched on the Empire by large numbers of Avars and Bulgars in the West, and Persians and Arabs in the East, the emperors found they had to supplement their professional forces with new levies raised among peasant proprietors and commanded by military governors called *strategoi*. To give such a militia an incentive, peasant tenures were made freehold, and their alienation to larger landholders was forbidden. This system, inaugurated by the Heraclians and perfected by the Isaurians, meant in effect that the whole weight of the Empire's administration was used to prevent anything like a system of proto-feudalism from developing. In the Roman world, east of Italy, nothing of the system that came to prevail in western Europe developed. Not until the ninth century was the large landed proprietor to become an important military or social factor in the Empire.

Religious Changes

SPREAD OF CHRISTIANITY INTO PAGAN AREAS

Although by 565 both the Franks and the Irish had accepted Christianity, most of northern Europe still remained pagan. In the late sixth century this began to change, as a result of the work of the Celtic Church in Britain, and of a new policy of conversion inaugurated by the Papacy. Irish monks established a center at Iona from which they converted Scotland, and then spread south into Northumbria, where they began the conversion of northern England. At about the same time, Pope Gregory the Great sent a band of Benedictine monks to the court of King Aethelbert of Kent. Their mission was successful, and Roman Christianity became firmly established at Canterbury. During the rest of the seventh century, from both Northumbria and Kent, Christianity penetrated the rest of Anglo-Saxon England. There were setbacks, particularly in the Midlands, where Penda's Mercia proved to be a center of pagan reaction. There was also considerable rivalry between Roman Christianity and that of the Celtic Church. Not until the King of Northumbria chose the former instead of the latter, at the Council of Whitby in 664, did this rivalry come to an end. By 718 England was Christian; a vigorous Anglo-Saxon Church, which combined elements of Celtic and Roman Christianity, had come into being.

During these years, Irish monks were also active on the continent. They entered Frankish domains to found monasteries throughout Gaul and even in Italy, where these establishments did much to convert the pagan countryside. Other Celtic monks moved into Germany, especially Bavaria, and even as far as Bohemia, where a residual Celtic-speaking population existed. Meanwhile Benedictine monasticism was also spreading north from Italy. Where the two forms met, friction developed, as had been the case in England, but in areas of northern France and the Rhinelands a certain amalgamation took place.

Finally, toward the beginning of the eighth century, Anglo-Saxon monks began to join their Irish brethren in missionary efforts on the continent. Since they spoke a Germanic tongue, they were especially attracted to Frisia and central Germany beyond the Rhine. Backed by the newly powerful Carolingian Mayors of the Palace, they began the conversion of this area, although it was not until the time of Boniface that their efforts were crowned with success.

Thus, by the early eighth century, a combination of Irish, Benedictine, and Anglo-Saxon missionary efforts had already profoundly altered the relationship between pagan and Christian in northwestern Europe, by converting all the peoples of the British Isles and of the kingdom of the Franks as far as the Rhine-Danube line. They had also begun to penetrate Frisia and central Germany and to lay the basis for future expansion.

The Eastern or Greek Church, on the other hand, gave little evidence during these years of similar missionary interest. Perhaps it found itself paralyzed by the internal religious conflicts that were brought on by Monothelitism. At any rate, it not only made no effort to convert nearby Slavs, Avars, or Bulgars, it even neglected the Kazars, who were close allies of the Empire. The latter, during this period, seem to have embraced Judaism instead, and even Islam made headway among them. Two centuries and more were to elapse before Cyril and Methodius would spread the gospel among Byzantium's pagan neighbors, as Columba, Columban, and Winfred were doing in the West.

TRIUMPH OF ORTHODOXY IN THE WEST

The second important development within the European Church was the triumph of Orthodoxy. One aspect of this was the final disappearance of Arianism, already weakened by Frankish conquest of the Arian Burgundians, and by Justinian's destruction of the Arian Ostrogoths and Vandals. Despite this, the Visigoths and Lombards continued to cling to Arian beliefs until, during the pontificate of Gregory, all of the former and some of the latter abandoned this heresy. By the mid-seventh century, the rest of the Lombards followed suit, and Orthodoxy reigned supreme in Western Europe.

On the other hand, religious unity was weakened by a series of theological controversies between the Papacy and the Latin West, on the one hand, and the emperors of Constantinople, on the other. The first of these, involving Justinian's attempt to force a religious compromise of his own choosing upon a reluctant Papacy, has already been mentioned. Justinian's formula was abandoned by his immediate successors, and an uneasy religious peace was maintained between Popes and emperors down to the time of Heraclius.

In Heraclius' last days, however, the emperor, who was struggling with the perennial problem of finding a compromise between the Orthodoxy of Chalcedon and the Monophysitism of his Eastern subjects, reopened the controversy with Rome by attempting to set up Monothelitism. The Papacy and the Latin West rejected this as heretical, and sheltered Eastern churchmen who shared that view. Heraclius, busy with Arab invasions, was able to do little to punish Rome for its defiance. Later on, however, when Constans II arrived in Italy with a large army, things were different: Constans seized the defiant Pope Martin and carried him into exile. None of this was to any avail, however, for Constans was murdered in Sicily, and his successor Constantine IV finally abandoned Monothelitism in 681. By 718, then, the religious struggle between Popes and Monothelite emperors had ended in a victory for the former. Orthodoxy, as defined at Chalcedon, had been successfully upheld by the Papacy, whose prestige was enhanced by this victory.

GROWTH OF MONASTICISM

In the East, monasticism suffered to some extent during the Monothelite controversy, since most of those who opposed that heresy were monastic figures. When Orthodoxy triumphed in 681, however, monasticism regained its strength. In the West, a more complex situation existed. Here, as noted earlier, three separate monastic traditions existed: a Celtic one, an anti-intellectual, ascetic one at Lerins and other southern European cloisters, and a Benedictine form at Monte Cassino. Both Celtic and Benedictine forms expanded during this period, the former into England and throughout the Continent, the latter into Lombard, Frankish, and Anglo-Saxon domains. During this expansion, Benedictine monasticism, as modified by Gregory the Great, gradually replaced the Lerins type as the dominant form in southern Europe. Celtic monasticism was more resistant. Only gradually did the Benedictine form, with its emphasis upon discipline, prevail over the Celtic variety, with its emphasis on independence. By the late seventh century, however, the battle had been won in both Anglo-Saxon England and much of northern France and Germany. What emerged was a monasticism, Benedictine in form, that combined order and discipline with Celtic monasticism's vigor and emphasis upon scholarly endeavor.

The success of Western monasticism in all its forms during this period was due to the fact that a monastery, as a self-sufficient economic unit, was able to exist as part of the predominantly rural society of the time, and even to thrive, whereas a church of bishops and priests, still organized on the older urban pattern, found the maintenance of its existence difficult. Furthermore, where conversion was important, abbeys could serve as mission stations in the midst of a pagan society—which explains why monks were the most successful missionaries of the period. Lastly, the monastic life appealed to many thoughtful, educated men who found careers in the rude kingdoms of the period unappealing. No wonder men of great administrative talent, such as Gregory the Great, were attracted by its charms.

INCREASING IMPORTANCE OF THE PAPACY

As we have seen, the Papacy emerged successful in the Monothelite controversy, and a number of other circumstances contributed to increasing papal prestige during this period, among them the Pope's role in converting England and winning Visigothic Spain and Lombard Italy for Orthodoxy. Yet it would be a mistake to overestimate the importance of such papal successes, or to regard the pontificate of Gregory the Great as like those of either his predecessors or his immediate successors.

From 565 to 718, all the Popes lived in a part of Italy that was subject to the emperor at Constantinople. Although they often disagreed with the emperors' religious policies, they never questioned the role of the latter as heads of a Christian Empire of which they were a part. During much of this period, the Popes also needed Imperial protection against Lombard political encroachment and Lombard Arianism. On the other hand, they were able to enjoy a degree of independence in Rome, because the Byzantine governor of Italy, known as the exarch, lived in Ravenna. Gregory the Great, for instance, negotiated with the Lombards on his own initiative. Nevertheless, the tradition of Constantine and the Imperial tie remained so strong that even Monothelitism and the controversy it evoked could not shatter it. Down to 718, the Popes continued to look to Constantinople and its emperors as their political anchor in a dangerous and uncertain sea, and to minimize their dependence on such newly converted Orthodox regions in the West as Spain, the Frankish domains, or Britain.

It is indeed doubtful whether there was much recognition in Rome, except perhaps during the brief pontificate of Gregory I, of the fact that the Pope headed a Latin Western Church that was distinct from that of the Greek East. Throughout the entire seventh century and down to 718, Rome was more Greek than Latin, and so were its Popes, all of whom were of Greek or Syrian origin. Perhaps this was because the Persian and Arab invasions and the Monothelite controversy had caused a considerable number of Orthodox Greek churchmen to seek refuge in Rome. The result was a Papacy that was anything but Latin. Nor was this true only of Rome. Theodore of Tarsus and Hadrian showed the same Greek or North African element in a region as remote as Anglo-Saxon England. A Latin Christendom distinct from the Greek East had not yet emerged, and was not to emerge until Carolingian times. Thus, in emphasizing the growth of papal prestige during this period, we need to remember that this took place within an older framework, in which the heirs of St. Peter still regarded themselves as part of a Christendom headed by the Roman emperors in Constantinople.

Cultural Progress

THE EASTERN ROMAN WORLD

Culturally, this was a period in which Europe as a whole made considerable progress, as its civilization changed; yet this progress was neither total nor uniform. In the Eastern Roman world, down to the end of Heraclius' reign, culture remained vigorous. Agathias and Menander continued to write secular history, as Procopius had done before them, and in the early seventh century others showed an interest in chronicling their times. Then the picture changed, as Constantinople found itself subjected to Arab attacks and the attendant violent social changes. We know of no contemporary historian or chronicler of the years between 642 and 718. Even the controversies provoked by Monothelitism are known to us mainly from Western sources. Except for a few scattered "Saints' Lives," Byzantium produced little literature during this age of blood and iron.

On the other hand, there is some echo in law of the innovations that these Heraclian soldier-emperors introduced in order to protect what remained of their empire. Two of these law codes have survived, each very different from that of Justinian: a commercial code, the Rhodian Sea Law, and the initial draft of a rural code called The Farmers' Law. Written in Greek instead of Latin, they reveal some important changes in the way in which society was affected by the state, and show us a civilization that was inventive and intellectually alert, even when subjected to intense internal and external pressures.

SECULAR AND RELIGIOUS CULTURE IN THE WEST

The patterns of cultural development in western Europe, during this same period, were very different. In Italy, Justinian's wars and the Lombard invasions that followed them ruined the promise of intellectual revival that was apparent at Theodoric's court. It was not until the time of Gregory the Great that there was any revival of Italian intellectual vigor. Even then, it was largely confined to Rome, and, as the case of Gregory shows, its character had changed radically. Gregory's writings, such as his *Pastoral Care* and his voluminous letters, show us a man who was linked to Cassiodorus and the late Roman world by administrative skill and training. But they also reveal that he had no interest in either rhetoric or history. And when we examine his *Dialogues* and *Moralia*, we see a mind that is narrowly medieval in its religious thought, far removed from the ideas expressed by Boethius in his *Consolatio* a century earlier. Rome in this period was able to produce administrators, and schools in which to train churchmen and musicians, but little else of cultural merit.

After Gregory, the decline in Rome's intellectual life is marked, despite the influx of educated Greek churchmen. The *Gesta Pontificalis* (*Chronicle of the Popes*) continued to be written, and a certain administrative and musical tradition was maintained that was necessary to a functioning Papacy. Yet it is only when the Papacy reacted to the Monothelite heresy that we see any intellectual vigor displayed, and in this case mainly by expatriate Greek churchmen. Even Monte Cassino, plundered during the incessant Lombard troubles of the time, ceased for a period to exist. Rome possessed many books, which were later to attract Anglo-Saxon scholars, but few scholars were interested in using them.

In contrast to a torpid Rome, however, Lombard Italy began to exhibit by the late seventh century some interest in intellectual life, especially at the court of its kings at Pavia. One sign of this was the issuing of a Lombard Code of Laws by King Rothari, to which his successors made additions during the next few decades. Another was royal patronage. for writers and scholars and a zeal for arts and letters at this same court. No doubt nearby monasteries like Bobbio and Farfa, with their active program of using scribes to copy manuscripts, contributed to this revival. At any rate this part of Italy laid the basis for the work of Paul the Deacon and Peter of Pisa in the next century.

The pattern of intellectual life was quite different in Merovingian Gaul. Here, about the time of Justinian's death, educated Gallo-Roman magnates, who tended to monopolize church and administrative offices, began to influence royal courts. Thanks to such men, who represented some surviving traditions of late Roman secular culture, a certain revival took place. One manifestation was an interest in the writing of history. Gregory of Tours composed his *History of the Franks*, an attempt to glorify and explain Frankish history from the time of Clovis by emphasizing a narrow religious orthodoxy. In the seventh century, Gregory's narrative was continued in the disjointed and much debated *Chronicle of Fredegar*. More important was the work of the poet Fortunatus. Although he was an Italian by birth, he spent most of his life in Gaul, as part of an educated circle that centered in St. Radegonde's nunnery at Poitiers. His poetry, linked to the classical past by his excellent Latin, was a creative innovation, which foreshadowed aspects of later Carolingian verse and even that of the troubadours. Still another evidence of the intellectual interests of the period was the appearance of new written Germanic law codes. A revised edition of the Salic Law was issued, and so were codes of the Burgundians and Bavarians, thus providing for the non-Roman peoples of this kingdom something that paralleled the Latin laws used by the Roman element in the population.

Such manifestations of secular culture were more than matched by those of a more strictly religious character, especially the composition of "Saints' Lives." Indeed, the late sixth and seventh centuries seem to have been the heyday of this kind of literature in Merovingian domains. This reflects a society that was increasingly concerned with the religious side of life, but it has another facet as well. These biographies were often a kind of propaganda, which emphasized the importance of the Merovingian family by stressing its holiness, especially that of its ladies. And when the Carolingians began to gain in importance, one of the first signs of their emerging eminence was the appearance of "Saints' Lives" celebrating the sanctity of members of this house, from St. Arnulf of Metz onward.

After Dagobert's death, however, symptoms of intellectual decline, which match those of seventh-century Byzantium, become evident in Gaul. As the center of gravity moved toward Austrasia, intellectual pursuits lost their importance. Marculf was still interested enough in a dying administrative tradition to gather documents for his *Formulary;* an inadequate Neustrian Chronicle attempted to continue the historical narratives of Gregory of Tours and Fredegar; but we sense a society that had come to the end of the older late Roman secular tradition. Only a few scattered monasteries under Celtic influence kept alive a spark of learning for the future.

Visigothic Spain presents still a third cultural pattern, more like that of Lombard Italy than that of Merovingian Gaul. Here, after a sixth century with little to show except in law, the seventh reveals more intellectual vigor. As Visigothic rulers became more powerful (one evidence is the great church councils they were able to convene), we find them encouraging intellectual life at their court and among the secular clergy. There was a considerable development of Visigothic law, which was increasingly influenced by late Roman legal principles, while church law developed too, judging from the canons of its councils. There was also a growth of a native Spanish literary and historical tradition. John of Biclar, Julian of Toledo, and Isidore of Seville all produced historical works of some importance, while the latter in his *Etymologies* maintained something of the late Roman secular tradition of rhetoric. Indeed, in some ways, seventh-century Spain represents the last flowering of the late Roman secular tradition in its older form. Nor was this ended when, early in the eighth century, Spain was conquered by the Moors, for right down to the conquest, something of the old urban life and aristocratic intellectual tradition of Rome lingered on in Spain.

In the British Isles, as in Spain, the sixth century saw little intellectual life, except for the composition of a few "Saints' Lives" and the establishment of schools in Celtic monasteries. By the seventh century,

however, the picture began to change, as the arrival of
Irish monks and cultured Benedictines helped produce
a quickening of intellectual vigor; this made Anglo-
Saxon England a cultural center that rivaled in importance those of Lombard Italy and Visigothic Spain.

Some of this intellectual vigor was reflected in a
secular tradition, using the Anglo-Saxon vernacular,
which resulted in that first compilation of Anglo-Saxon
law, the *Laws of Ine*, and in the appearance of the
epic poem *Beowulf*, which celebrated the Teutonic
past of its people. More important, though, was the
work of "the Venerable Bede," who in his monastery
at Jarrow composed in Latin his *Ecclesiastical History
of the English People*. It was the best history written
during the early Middle Ages, and told how England
was Christianized. Bede, although a monumental figure,
was no isolated one. He had Anglo-Saxon and Irish
contemporaries, such as Adamnan, who wrote the *Life
of St. Columban*, and others who began to chronicle
the heroic efforts of English monks to convert the
heathen people of Frisia and Germany. Adamnan
even compiled a standard guide for pilgrims visiting
the Holy Land. Within a century after its conversion,
then, England had become a center of culture that
was already beginning to influence the nearby Continent.

One peculiarity of Irish and Anglo-Saxon intellectual
development, however, deserves particular mention. It
was a development almost completely confined to the
cloister, rather than centering in the royal courts or
among the secular clergy. This made it more narrowly
Christian than the intellectual life we find in late-
sixth-century Gaul or in seventh-century Spain. It thus
had little interest in the late Roman tradition of rhetoric that had attracted Cassiodorus, Isidore of Seville,

or even Gregory of Tours. And it was this narrower tradition that was passed on to the Carolingian world, which it was to influence so profoundly in the late eighth century.

ARCHITECTURE AND ART

This was not a great age of building in Europe, and few examples of its architecture have survived. A Byzantium fighting for its life could build little, and only a few small churches in Rome show that the basilican plan continued to be used, linking its architecture with that of the late Roman world. At Fréjus and Poitiers in Gaul, we find a few examples of baptisteries that date from these years. It is only in Visigothic Spain that we find a distinctive style of architecture, although even the examples that have survived show us that Spain, despite the use of the horseshoe arch, still followed late Roman and Byzantine traditions.

A survey of the art of the period reveals a greater range. Mosaics from Salonika and Rome show that the Byzantine style, as developed by Justinian's time, continued to attract artists, while sarcophagi and ivories produced in the East Roman world, in Italy, and in Aquitaine show a continuing classical tradition among craftsmen. We even have an extraordinary series of frescos by an unknown artist in a small north Italian church at Castelseprio, which reveal a creativity that had assimilated the classical tradition and yet was able to present something completely new. Nor did Visigothic Spain lag artistically, as one can see by examining the magnificent crowns and jewels that have been preserved in the treasury of the Cathedral of Toledo.

More interesting, perhaps, than these artistic works, which reveal a continuing late Roman and Byzantine

canon of taste, are signs of a barbarian tradition of
art in northern Europe. Here the magnificent Sutton
Hoo treasure, which dates from the early seventh century, like the Kentish jewelry that has survived, shows
that Anglo-Saxon craftsmen continued to follow a style
derived from an earlier age in Germany and Scandinavia.
Equally impressive is Frankish ornamentation, which,
as Salin has shown, came from four different ateliers in
northern Gaul and is also definitely part of this barbarian tradition. Nor can we ignore the metalwork of
Vendel Sweden, which reveals a similar artistic sensibility.

Equally important is Celtic art, as shown in the
illuminated manuscripts of the period, such as the
Book of Durrow, which deeply influenced Anglo-Saxon
scribal artists. The same Celtic tradition lies behind
the crosses that are found in many parts of the British
Isles, and the numerous Ogham stones discovered in
many areas in Scotland. Celtic, German barbarian,
classical, and Byzantine artistic traditions all continued
to show a vitality throughout these years and to link
this nascent civilization with those that had preceded
it.

Summary

This was not a period of cultural decadence for Europe
as a whole, although the late seventh century saw the
late Roman secular world gradually disappear in its
older form in Byzantium, Italy, and Gaul, while the
Moorish conquest brought it to an end in Spain. The
Latin of Gregory of Tours is indeed barbarous, and Isidore of Seville's *Etymologies* are but a decadent echo
of Pliny the Elder. But this is only part of the story.

As the old world of Roman law, culture, and art decayed, we can see a new vigor in many parts of Europe. New law codes in Byzantium, in Frankish domains, in Lombard Italy, in Visigothic Spain, and in Anglo-Saxon England testify to a living interest in the law. The writing of historical works in these same regions indicates the existence of a growing educated class that was concerned with the immediate past. A continuation of earlier artistic styles shows an artistic sensibility that had not been dulled, but remained fresh and lively. Meanwhile a Christian culture was developing in the cloisters that was laying the foundation of the medieval European civilization of the future. Much of Europe was still rural and remote, as compared with more advanced areas in the rest of the world. Its governments seem rudimentary, as compared with those of the Roman Empire that had preceded them. But in a cultural, economic, and social sense, Europe had begun to move toward a new period.

chapter III

The Carolingian Era,

A.D. 718–840

*B*etween 718 and 840, there emerged in Europe a state that can at last be regarded as distinctly European—the Carolingian Empire. It is true that many elements that were to be part of historical Europe were not included in it. Spain with its Moorish traditions, the British Isles and Scandinavia, most of Slavic eastern Europe and the Balkans, with their heritage from Byzantium—all these lay beyond the regions over which Charlemagne ruled. Indeed, it would be mistaken to assert that, in the year 800, Aix-la-Chapelle was more European than Constantinople. Even during these years, Europe was more than the Carolingian Empire.

Nevertheless, the Carolingian era was more distinctly European than any that had preceded it. Hitherto, Europe had had no existence distinct from that of wider non-European areas of culture. For centuries, much of it had been part of a Roman-Mediterranean region, in which parts of North Africa and the Near East had played an important role. The remainder—what we have called "barbarian"—was also part of a larger area, which did not stop at the Urals, but extended eastward to the borders of China. Chinese activities directed against nomadic peoples on their frontiers could thus set off a chain reaction that affected the entire complexion of barbarian Europe at the other edge of the steppes.

But by 718 this was no longer the case. The rise of Islam had been followed by the Moslem conquest of Syria, Egypt, North Africa, and Spain, which separated almost all of civilized Europe from the Mediterranean area of which it had long been a part. At about the same time, a generally less recognized event—the rise of the Kazar kingdom in south Russia—effectively created a barrier between the barbarian tribes of Central Asia and those who lived in central and eastern Europe. Thus, for the first time, civilized Europe, with its heritage of Romano-Byzantine civilization, and barbarian Europe, with its distinctive traditions, became isolated from regions that had long profoundly influenced their destinies. As this was happening, there arose in western Europe a Carolingian Empire that formed a center in which Roman and barbarian traditions could mingle in a new way, and which, even though it was ephemeral, helped lay the groundwork for a new Europe.

Emergence of the Carolingian Empire

The Carolingian Empire, which became the most important political entity of the period, was not com-

pletely new. Initially, it was simply the old kingdom
of the Merovingians, "under new management." As
time went on, and its borders were extended, it changed
its character. By absorbing the Lombard kingdom, the
exarchate of Ravenna, the duchy of Rome, Gascony,
Septimania, the Spanish March, Saxony, and the Slavic
borderlands to the east, it became multinational. The
peoples of these regions, who had never been part of
the Merovingian realm, now became part of the Carolingian Empire. During the same period, the Carolingian rulers also developed their power in such a way
that it came to be based on a separate Western church,
under joint Carolingian and papal control hostile to
Byzantium. This led directly to the claim that their
realm was an "empire," equal to the legitimate Roman
Empire with its capital in Constantinople.

The two other effective political powers in Europe
that were strong enough to rival this empire were the
Moslem emirate of Cordova and the Roman Empire
of Constantinople. The former emerged as politically
independent of the Abassid caliphs of Baghdad about
the middle of the eighth century. For some decades
after its establishment as a separate state by Abd-ar-Rahman I, it was torn by civil strife, as Arab factions,
Berbers, and newly converted Spanish Moslems battled
for a place in its political and social structure. Despite
these disorders, it proved to be strong enough to keep
independent Spanish Christian princes from advancing
south of the Douro, and it limited Carolingian conquests to a region just north of the Ebro. Although the
majority of its inhabitants remained Christian, its
Moslem upper classes were culturally part of an Islamic
world that stretched from the Atlantic to Central Asia.
This had the effect of separating Moslem Spain from
the rest of Europe.

The Roman Empire, now often loosely termed Byzantine, was a far more important factor. Its able Isaurian emperors and their immediate successors continued to hold Sicily, as well as parts of southern Italy and Venice, and maintained a protectorate over the Lombard principality of Benevento. They controlled coastal regions of the Balkans, and were powerful enough to regain parts of Greece from the Slavs who occupied them, as well as to continue exercising an influence over the Bulgars and the Kazars. Their navy, which continued to be strong, gave Byzantium considerable power in the waters about Italy and in the western Mediterranean. At the same time, the Iconoclast heresy, which the Empire professed during most of this period, had the effect of alienating much of the Latin West. It pushed the Papacy into the arms of Frankish protectors, and was an important factor in the chain of events that ended in the proclamation of a Western Empire that rivaled the legitimate Empire in Constantinople.

OTHER STATES IN EUROPE

Beyond the frontiers of Moslem Spain, Byzantium, and the Carolingian Empire lay other states that had developed some degree of political cohesion. In northwestern Spain, soon after 740, several independent Christian principalities arose which we will know, a century later, as Leon, Navarre, and Aragon; their character was essentially Spanish, different from that of either the emirate of Cordova or the Carolingian Empire.

In England, the vague hegemony exercised earlier by Kent or Northumbria was succeeded by the more extensive authority of Offa of Mercia and Egbert of

Wessex. Offa's domination of most of England resulted in a greater emphasis on internal order, reform of the coinage, and an effort to establish commercial and diplomatic relations with the Carolingian Empire.

The same trend is noticeable in Scandinavia, where a Danish royal house arose that was capable of building a wall called the Danwerke across the Jutland peninsula to check the Carolingian advance; it was also able to muster its ships south to attack Carolingian shores. At the time of Louis the Pious, representatives of this house entered into close diplomatic relations with Aix-la-Chapelle. In Sweden, as we learn from an account of St. Anskar's visit to Uppsala, a similar kingdom was beginning to emerge. Neither Danish nor Swedish kings had been able to establish order within their domains by 840, but they were at least making an effort to do so.

In central and eastern Europe, there was the same tendency toward greater political cohesion, especially after Charlemagne had destroyed the Avar state about 800. With Avar power ended, a Greater Moravia began to emerge, just north of the middle Danube; it may have had some links with the earlier principality of Samo. More important was the powerful Bulgarian state that developed along the lower Danube. Fashioned by Tervel in the first years of the eighth century, this kingdom survived campaigns directed against it by Constantine V, to emerge as a powerful rival of Byzantium in the Balkans. Its armies defeated those of Constantinople in the field, and spread its dominion over the northern and central portion of the Balkan Peninsula. Finally, we have the powerful Kazar kingdom just north of the Caucasus, which defended itself against Abassid attacks and expanded its authority, until it dominated much of the steppelands of southern Russia.

EXPANSION AND DECLINE

By 840, therefore, the line of civilization, as exemplified by politically organized areas, had moved beyond the point it had reached in 718, and the bases had been laid for further progress. Moreover, extension was accompanied by political consolidation and the development of political organization. For example, by the time of Louis the Pious (815–840), the Carolingian Empire bore little resemblance to that which Charles Martel had ruled a century earlier. In Charles' time, the Carolingians had controlled little more than Austrasia and Neustria, while outlying regions, such as Bavaria, Alemannia, Aquitaine, and Provence, were under the control of hereditary princes, often called dukes. Charles Martel and his son Pepin eliminated these competitors and added their territory to their realm, while simultaneously dealing with such dangerous neighbors as the Frisians, the Lombards, and the Moslems of Septimania. By the end of Pepin's reign, the task had been completed except in Bavaria. Then Charlemagne extended Carolingian frontiers still further, to include Gascony and the Spanish March, northern and central Italy, Bavaria and Saxony, and the Slavic lands bordering eastern Germany.

Yet even Charlemagne's program of expansion had its limits. He was unable to conquer Saragossa and the Ebro valley, and his control over Gascony and Brittany remained superficial. In Italy, his attempts to absorb Venice and Benevento were thwarted by Byzantium. Despite his conquest of Saxony, Denmark resisted him successfully. Finally, by failing to develop an adequate navy, he allowed the Vikings to control the waters of the North Sea, and the Byzantines to remain masters of the western Mediterranean.

The reign of his son, Louis, saw much of this work undone, since the latter lacked his father's military and administrative talents. The Empire's frontiers began to contract, as parts of Gascony and the Spanish March were lost, and no effective measures were taken against Viking enemies. Later in Louis' reign, a series of civil wars took place that further weakened the Empire. By 843, the Carolingian Empire had been subdivided, and was subject to internal disorders that encouraged Viking and Moslem enemies to attack it with a large degree of impunity.

RELATIONSHIPS WITH CHURCH AND LANDOWNER

While the Carolingian Empire was going through a political development that saw it grow slowly in strength and then swiftly decline, it was also finding a special relationship with the Western Church. From almost their earliest period of power, the Carolingians —unlike the Merovingians—relied upon the Church as one of the bases of their authority. Thus Charles Martel and Pepin, despite their ruthless appropriation of Church lands, backed Boniface and others in their efforts to extend Christianity into heathen Frisia and central Germany. Pepin went on to ally himself with the Papacy and to protect the Popes against the Lombards, in return for papal backing in deposing the last Merovingians and proclaiming the Carolingians kings of the Franks. Thereafter, they ruled as much in the capacity of God's and the Church's earthly representatives as they did in the capacity of rulers who owed their dominion to force of arms. During the reign of Charlemagne, this policy led to the conquest of northern and central Italy, and the Pope's crowning of this ruler as emperor in the year 800.

The other basis of the Empire was a fighting aristocracy of landowners, who supported the Carolingians in return for booty, land, and political office. During the seventh century, it was this nobility, who could afford the heavy expense of war horses and equipment, that had doomed the Merovingian state to weakness. Now they became the bulwark of Carolingian power. At first recruited primarily from Austrasian noble families, as the Empire advanced its borders they were joined by other noble landowners, such as the Goths of Septimania, until they became a more cosmopolitan group. Although they remained loyal to Charlemagne, it was Louis' failure to control them that made his reign and those of his sons unsuccessful. For Carolingian dominion over much of western Europe, which owed so much to the swords of this fighting nobility, proved unable to survive the lack of support that they displayed later on.

INSTITUTIONS OF GOVERNMENT

A final point worth noting about this Empire is its lack of self-perpetuating institutions of government. None of the Carolingians possessed enough money to pay armies or administrators in any way except in land. Thus they were forced either to employ churchmen as administrators, or to use nobles as governors of local districts, the latter being paid in land and the profits of office. Innovations such as the use of traveling officials called *missi*, or the creation of a local *scabini* element, composed of magnates who attended court and were used to check powerful officials, were only partially successful, as was the use of powerful abbots and bishops for the same general purpose. Similarly unsuccessful, over a long period, was the attempt to control the army and the officials they appointed by having them swear special oaths of fealty. None proved to be an adequate substitute for salaries in hard cash. Thus, toward the end of the reign of Louis the Pious, nobles were more and more tending to become alodial landholders, officials were ignoring instructions from Aix-la-Chapelle, and officeholding was becoming less a reward for loyal service than an hereditary family right. The Carolingian Empire was on the verge of dissolution, in a part of Europe that was open to both Viking and Moslem invaders.

The Byzantine Empire

GOVERNMENTAL REORGANIZATION

The story of the Byzantine Empire during these years was quite different. In 718 its new emperor, Leo the Isaurian, had just won a great victory over the Arab armies and navies that had been besieging Constantinople. During the next few decades, he and his able successor, Constantine V, cleared Arab armies out of Asia Minor and destroyed Arab sea power in a great battle off Cyprus. Constantine was equally victorious in the Balkans, where he blunted the power of the Bulgarians and reclaimed some areas of Greece from the Slavs.

At the same time, these soldier-emperors completed the reorganization of the army and government that had been begun by the Heraclians. They maintained the effective centralized bureaucracy of their predecessors, as well as the small professional army and navy stationed near Constantinople that was paid in money. In the provinces, they continued to combine military and administrative functions in themes that they put into the hands of strategoi, or generals. Even more than their predecessors, they relied for defense upon themal armed forces, composed of peasant soldiers and part-time sailors, whose freehold tenures they guaranteed against larger landowners, in order to ensure their zeal. Thus the overall pattern of the Isaurian government and army differed profoundly from that of the Carolingians. Whereas the latter was based on a class of larger landowners, who monopolized public office and provided elite troops, the Isaurians relied upon the small proprietor as the basis of their armed forces, which were stiffened by an elite, well-paid professional army and navy located near their capital. And while the Carolingians had to pay their administrators and elite cavalry in land in return for service, in Byzantium money was available for that purpose.

RELIGIOUS POLICY: THE PROBLEM OF ICONOCLASM

Byzantium also differed from the Carolingians in religious policy. As noted, the Carolingians relied upon the Church and maintained close and harmonious relations with it. In the Byzantine Empire, the Isaurian emperors adopted policies that led to the bitterly divisive struggle of Iconoclasm. This began when, in 726, Emperor Leo decided to ban the use of images. His iconoclastic decrees, although supported by the army and by Asia Minor, raised a storm in the rest of the Empire, and especially in Italy, where the Popes refused to enforce them.

When Leo died, his son Constantine V proved to be an even more zealous Iconoclast, and a violent program was adopted not only against the Papacy but against all monasteries within the Empire's borders, for monks were particularly opposed to Iconoclasm. As a result, many monks and clergy sought refuge in Italy, and the breach between the Popes and the emperor widened. Finally, when the Lombards took advantage of the situation to advance on Ravenna and Rome, which they had long coveted, the Papacy in desperation sought a new protector and allied itself with the Carolingians. First Pepin and then Charlemagne entered Italy at the head of strong armies in response to papal pleas for assistance. The results were momentous. Northern and central Italy became Carolingian, the Papacy and the Western Church broke with Constantinople, and a religious schism took place. Finally, in the year 800, a rival Carolingian Empire in the West was proclaimed. Now the Latin Christian West and the Greek Christian East eyed each other across a gulf of political and religious rivalry.

Once the break had taken place in the sphere of religion, political rivalry between the two empires maintained it, despite the Empress Irene's return to Orthodoxy in 787. And when Iconoclasm returned to favor in Byzantium a little while later, religious friction was added to that in the political sphere. On the whole, however, it seems probable that the reluctance of Byzantium to recognize, except in grudging fashion, the Carolingian claim to an Imperial title was the chief reason why relations between the two Empires remained strained and why the schism continued.

MILITARY DEVELOPMENTS

Iconoclasm, however, did more than precipitate a political and religious break between East and West. It also had serious results for the Empire itself. Because the more Greek areas tended to be iconodule, that is, to support the veneration of images, they suffered serious persecution from Iconoclast emperors.

And since these same areas were those in which the main provincial themal fleets were located, this affected the Empire's naval strength. Thus, by the early ninth century, Byzantium's naval defenses had lost their effectiveness; after the revolt of Thomas the Slav in the 820s, this deficiency allowed Moslem flotillas a relatively free hand in attacking Crete and Sicily, which began to transform the Mediterranean into a Moslem d— sea.

At the same time, Byzantine arm— disorders, also lost their earlier e— may have been due in part to a ch— policy, which no longer protected s— ures, and thus made peasant soldiers le— defending their localities. The result, fr— Irene, was an empire that was increasi— Arab and Bulgar incursions, which cou— only by heavy money payments.

In the early ninth century, however, form of the army took place. The Emper— abandoned Heraclian and Isaurian relianc— soldiers and turned to a heavily armed ca— elite arm. This change favored the large and facilitated their rise as the dominant countryside. Thus belatedly there began to Byzantium a fighting aristocracy of landown— to that in the Carolingian Empire—a de— that was to have an important effect upon t of the Byzantine Empire.

Economic Changes

We have already noted how the last years of the seventh century saw an almost revolutionary change in the pattern of European economic life. By 750, this had resulted in a Europe that was divided into five distinct local economic regions, in contrast to its earlier tendency toward overall economic unity: the first of these regions was Moslem Spain; the second was the Carolingian Empire, and its borderlands of northern Christian Spain, the British Isles, and Scandinavia; the third was composed of the Byzantine Empire and most of Italy; the fourth took in Central Europe; and the fifth and last was a region that stretched from Kazaria to the Baltic, and included much of eastern Scandinavia as well.

THE BYZANTINE EMPIRE AND ITALY

Of all these regions, that which included the Byzantine Empire and Italy was economically the most advanced in the year 750. Constantinople remained a great cosmopolitan city, containing considerable industry and connected with the wider world by extensive commercial contacts. Its gold nomisma was still maintained throughout the Empire, although by the early ninth century parts of southern Italy had begun to use a lighter gold coin known as the *mancus*. Byzantium traded with the Carolingian Empire and northwestern Europe by way of Venice, with western Moslem Mediterranean areas via Naples and Sicily, with Bulgaria and Central Europe by way of Saloniki, and with Kazaria via Cherson. Trade with the Moslem silver dirhem and gold dinar areas of the Near East centered in Constantinople, Trebizond, and trading centers on the borders of Syria. Byzantium thus maintained its role as a middleman, linking areas of Europe with Asia and reaping rich rewards in the process.

Although this helps to explain Byzantium's continuing prosperity, it does seem probable that the overall volume of trade was considerably less than it had been earlier. This was largely due to a deliberate policy of prohibiting the export of gold, and forbidding Byzantine merchants to trade with the outside world except at designated trade portals. A decrease in trade volume was perhaps also the result of the wars and hostility between Byzantium and her neighbors that periodically interrupted commercial intercourse. Whatever the cause, the result was to limit the Empire's commercial contacts with every other part of Europe except Italy.

Within the Empire, Isaurian policies, which favored the smallholder over the large landowner, led to rural prosperity in much of Asia Minor and in those parts of Thrace where such farmers were able to sell their agricultural produce at a good price in the great city of Constantinople. But this situation was beginning to change. The revolt led by Thomas the Slav was probably the result of a steady encroachment of large landowners on peasant tenures, which was no longer restrained by Imperial policy. The reconquest of certain areas in Greece and Macedonia during these years may also have encouraged a certain agricultural revival in these parts of the Empire and made Saloniki a more important trading center. Other than this, we have little knowledge of economic conditions.

MOSLEM SPAIN

Our knowledge of economic conditions in Moslem Spain is also limited. A Moslem silver dirhem coinage was used, similar to that used in Tunis, Algeria, and Morocco. Urban life continued, and many Jews continued to live in the towns and cities. At this time a large number of Moors from North Africa and Arabs from the Near East migrated into the Iberian Peninsula, bringing with them a distinctive husbandry adapted to semiarid lands, and a system of irrigation that spread through Andalusia and Valencia. These years apparently also saw the end of the old Roman villa system. These changes, which caused considerable social stress, adversely affected Spain's prosperity, as did the struggles between Arab and Berber factions in Abd-ar-Rahman's time and civil strife a little later in such cities as Toledo and Cordova, where newly converted Moslems sought equality with their Arab masters. Similarly upsetting to the economy was the expulsion of thousands of these converts to Fez in Morocco and distant Alexandria.

By 840, a Moslem Spain had emerged that was quite different from that of late Roman and Visigothic times. Its older Roman pattern of socioeconomic life had disappeared. Now its essential links were with Moslem North Africa, which it came to resemble in many respects, as its agriculture and urban life changed. Although a few of its Moslem and Jewish merchants traded silks and spices for slaves and other products from Carolingian domains, by way of Catalonia and southern French ports, its important economic connections were those it maintained with the great Moslem-controlled trading area that was now emerging between Gibraltar and the borders of Turkestan.

CENTRAL EUROPE

The Central European region, from the Baltic to the mountains of the Balkan Peninsula, was probably the most primitive, underdeveloped part of Europe. It lay east of a relatively underdeveloped area of the Carolingian Empire, and south and east of even more primitive regions of the Baltic and western Russia.

Furthermore, the Avars had blocked trade routes passing through this region for centuries, while Byzantine trade policies also hindered economic development. It was only after Charlemagne had destroyed the power of the Avars, in about 800, that outside commerce reached this part of Europe, and then it was only a trickle from the Carolingian Empire.

During these years no trading places emerged anywhere in the region, and its economy remained local and agricultural. On the other hand, recent archeological studies show that there was considerable agrarian development at this time, as the Slavs cut down the forests and cleared fields for agriculture. Although this activity had only local significance immediately, it laid the foundations for future growth, and for the entry of Central Europe into the general stream of European economic life, by enabling it to provide exports other than the slaves that had been its chief contribution during the Carolingian era.

FROM KAZARIA TO THE BALTIC

The region that stretched from the land of the Kazars north to the Baltic was much more favorably placed. It enjoyed a link with gold-rich Byzantium, by way of Cherson, that stimulated its commerce. More important were its economic connections with Iraq, Persia, and Turkestan to the south and east. From this region, a growing current of commerce flowed north from Baghdad, Ré, Isfahan, Bokhara, and other centers, until it reached the Baltic by way of the Volga and Russia's northern river system. Along these trade routes silks, spices, silver, and industrial wares were exchanged for slaves, furs, honey, beeswax, and even swords. Such commerce was important enough to make the Kazars, who were the principal intermediaries, wealthy and powerful. It laid the economic foundations of the Kievan state that was soon to appear, by creating such cities as Itil in Kazaria and such centers as Kiev, Polotsk, Smolensk, and Old Ladoga in Russia. And it brought with it hoards of silver dirhems, which have been found as far north as Gotland and the Swedish mainland. By 840, it had made that part of Europe almost an extension of the great Islamic dirhem trading area that stretched from Iraq to the borders of India and China.

THE CAROLINGIAN EMPIRE

The last localized economic region, which centered in the Carolingian Empire, was the most important of all. About this, we have more information. Its heartland was an area between the Loire and the Rhine, including certain areas of southeastern England and Frisia. This area was linked to Italy by way of Alpine passes, but it was more dependent upon local commerce that had developed about the northern seas. As decades passed and Charlemagne expanded his Empire, this nucleus grew until, by 820, it came to include within its borders all of France, northwestern Spain, and a large part of the British Isles. Denmark, western Norway, and areas in Sweden and Germany east of the Rhine were part of its hinterland, while northern and central Italy, now Carolingian, were more closely linked to it in an economic sense. At the same time, northwestern Europe began to lose its economic isolation. By way of Venice and northern Italy, it traded with the Byzantine world; via Gotland and Uppland Sweden, with the Kazarian-Russian area; by way of southern France, with the Moslem West; and via eastern Germany and the upper Danube, it established commercial contacts with Central Europe. (See Map 3.)

Gradually, as all this happened, the Carolingian-centered economic region developed special characteristics. One was a common silver coinage, based on the Carolingian silver penny that Pepin and Charlemagne had established as a standard of value for their Empire, and which Offa of Mercia and Egbert of Wessex copied in their English domains. Coin hoards show that Carolingian money reached Norway, Denmark, and Avar lands in some quantities. Since they were quite similar to the Moslem silver dirhem that was used in Spain, Sweden, and the Baltic, they could easily be exchanged for the latter. On the other hand, except in Italy, the Carolingians did not coin gold prior to the reign of Louis the Pious; this suggests that there may have been some difficulties in trading with the Byzantine world, which remained on the gold standard. The Carolingians did issue a special gold coin, but finds of this money suggest that it circulated only about the North Sea, far from the Byzantine nomisma and Moslem gold dinar areas.

A second feature of this economic area was that, by the early ninth century, its heartland had become relatively industrialized. Much of its trade therefore consisted of industrial wares, such as the cloth of England and Flanders; swords, glass, and metalware from the Rhinelands, Belgium, and northern France; and iron, copper, tin, and silver, produced in a number of mining regions. Natural products, however, also figured in its commerce—such as wheat, wine, timber, honey, fish, and furs. Most of these wares were highly prized in the Baltic, where they arrived in significant volume, as well as in areas as remote as the Moslem

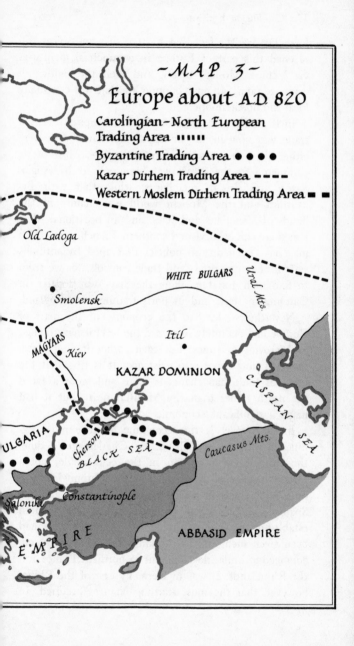

-MAP 3-
Europe about AD 820

Carolingian-North European
Trading Area ▮▮▮▮▮
Byzantine Trading Area ●●●●
Kazar Dirhem Trading Area ----
Western Moslem Dirhem Trading Area ▬ ▬

Old Ladoga

WHITE BULGARS

Smolensk

Ural Mts.

Itil

MAGYARS

Kiev

KAZAR DOMINION

CASPIAN SEA

ULGARIA

Cherson

BLACK SEA

Caucasus Mts.

aloniki

Constantinople

EMPIRE

ABBASID EMPIRE

East. Despite the fact that Eastern silks and spices still reached this part of Europe in commercial quantities via Venice, Moslem Spain, and even the Baltic, all evidence points to an economic life that was essentially local and northern-oriented.

In the third place, the Carolingian Empire's external trade was now in the hands of merchants who were either alien to it or lived on its borders. Most of its commerce to the north was monopolized by Anglo-Saxon and Frisian merchants, while that with Byzantium and the Moslem world was mainly in the hands of Venetians and Jews, and an occasional Moslem merchant who visited southern French ports. This may have been due to policies that aped Byzantium's system of trade portals and trade controls, for we seem to find such a system along the Slav-Avar frontier, in Carolingian Italy, and in ports trading with England.

Nevertheless, by 840 the economy of this part of Europe had definitely surpassed the level it had reached in Merovingian times. For each earlier trading place, two had now come into existence. It is true that the focus of trade had changed: more and more it faced the north rather than the Mediterranean; but it had made a significant economic advance.

In no respect is this economic advance more significant than in agriculture. By Charlemagne's time, the agricultural revolution in the countryside, noted earlier, had spread over much of the Carolingian Empire. Now tracts of wasteland in Septimania and the Spanish March began to be cultivated by Church establishments and by individual magnates who had been given such land by the king. The government encouraged a similar development in northern France and the Rhinelands. It was in Germany east of the Rhine, however, that the most startling changes occurred. In the valley of the Main and along the upper Danube, forests began to disappear and cultivated fields took their place. The same process was going on beyond the Empire's frontiers, in those parts of Wessex and Mercia that were close to the Celtic borderlands, in Spain just north of the Douro, and in Slavic Central Europe.

This deforestation and clearing of the soil was often accompanied by the spread of the heavy, wheeled plough, along with other technological improvements noted earlier. The results are seen in the fascinating sketch of an agricultural estate that is known as the *Polytype of Abbot Irminon*, and some idea of how rural manors were handled administratively can be obtained from Charlemagne's own capitulary *de Villis*, which describes this Carolingian ruler's private estates. Certain things, such as the spread of a more efficient three-field system, still lay in Europe's future; but by 840, in northern Spain, Britain, and the Carolingian Empire, monasteries and private proprietors alike were beginning to change the agricultural face of Europe.

Technological improvements were not confined to agriculture. The stirrup, introduced earlier, now became so widespread that it revolutionized warfare on the continent. Its use by Carolingian *vassi dominici*, as royal vassals were called, probably explains the ability of the latter to defeat Lombards, Moslems, and other enemies in battle, and its employment by the Bulgars may well have forced Byzantium to shift the emphasis from foot soldiers to heavily armed cavalrymen early in the ninth century. Similarly, the pattern-welded swords of the Rhinelands spread over a wider area of northern and eastern Europe; an Arab geographer tells of their being sent as prized articles of commerce to the trade marts of the Moslem East. Like the pallia fresonica, the Frisian cloth of the Carolingians, they had a renown that was worldwide.

Perhaps the most spectacular example of the more advanced technology of this era was shipbuilding, as seen in the Scandinavian ships that were preserved intact in the royal graves near Oslo. One of them, the Gokstad ship, is an oceangoing vessel, which shows how Vikings dared to brave the open sea of the North Atlantic to raid the shores of western Europe, and a little later to venture as far west as Iceland and Greenland. The fact that such ships could be built in a part of Europe so far removed from the advanced worlds of Byzantium and Islam is the supreme testimony to European technological skill in this period.

Although a small artisan and merchant class inhabited trading places from England eastward to Russia, north of Byzantium, Italy, and Spain, Europe was still predominantly rural. This meant that only two classes of any real importance existed: one was an upper class of large landowners; the other, a peasantry that worked the soil. Even more than in the preceding period, the class of large landowners was the dominant one, not only in the Carolingian Empire, but increasingly in the Byzantine Empire.

In Charlemagne's domains, the dominant role of this class of fighting landowners began to result in a political and social system that may be described as feudal. Earlier, they had bound lowly dependents to their persons by gifts of land and protection, in return for military and other service. Now the Carolingians themselves elevated such service and made it an honorable one, binding upon great magnates, office-holders, and churchmen to the crown. By Charlemagne's time, the emperor began to distribute land to such men in return for their oaths of fealty, thus creating ties that provided him with an army and an administrative cadre.

It must not be imagined, however, that such feudal ties were all-embracing by 840, even within the Carolingian Empire. They were most fully developed between the Rhine and the Loire. Most of Italy, southern France, and Germany still found them uncongenial, however, while in other parts of Europe, such as northwest Spain and Britain, they had only begun to develop. Here there existed a social distinction between an upper class of fighting men and a lower class of cultivators; but a network of feudal relations had not yet appeared. Even in Byzantium, such incipient feudalism as we find at the end of this period had hardly advanced beyond the Merovingian stage, in which magnates were starting to dominate their lowly neighbors. Everywhere, however, a new society was beginning to emerge, in some form, from which the feudalism of the future was to spring.

Relations with the Church

THE CAROLINGIAN EMPIRE

Major developments necessarily affected the Church. More settled government and the extension of cultivated land favored the expansion of Christianity. By the middle of the eighth century, Frisia and central Germany had been converted, while the establishment of monasteries and an episcopacy had begun to incorporate these regions into the hierarchical structure of Western Christendom. Some decades later, using a calculated brutality, Charlemagne completed the Christianization of Saxony, while along his southwest borders he coerced pagan Basques in a similar fashion. Soon after his death, his successor, Louis the Pious, used diplomacy and missionaries in an attempt to convert the Danes, while St. Anskar's mission began to spread Christianity to Sweden. By 840, the boundaries of Christendom had been considerably expanded in the West.

In the same part of Europe, there was also a considerable growth of monasticism. The Carolingians were in no small measure responsible for this, for they were generous in giving such establishments land and privileges and royal protection. The result was new monasteries built in Germany, and both the restoration of old ones and the building of new ones in southern France and Catalonia. Even in distant Italy, abbeys were the recipients of Imperial bounty; Monte Cassino, which lay on the boundaries of the Empire, served as a last refuge for a distinguished member of the Carolingian house. Louis the Pious assisted St. Benedict of Aniane in spreading his reformed Benedictine rule throughout the Empire, and the influence of such Anglo-Saxon reformers as Alcuin, with their insistence on education, improved the moral and religious tone of the monastic movement as a whole.

This monastic movement was not confined to Carolingian Europe. In Ireland, down to the time of the Viking attacks in the early ninth century, monasteries continued to play a decisive social and educational role, while in Britain they maintained their vigor for at least two or three generations after the death of Bede. Even in northwest Spain, the early ninth century saw a revival of interest in monasticism that matched the interest displayed by Carolingian Catalonia. Everywhere the monastery emerged as a special embodiment of Christianity, much prized by the Western Church.

Those years during which Christianity spread and

abbeys flourished saw no increase, however, in the power of the Papacy. In fact, there was a contrary trend. The Popes, it is true, took the lead in rejecting Iconoclasm, and broke with Constantinople to seek new protectors in the West. Once this had been accomplished, however, they found that they had taken leave of a distant master, only to find another nearby. Although Pepin gave the Popes the former Byzantine territories in central Italy—later to be known as the Papal States—after 774, Charlemagne disregarded his father's grant, annexed these lands to his empire, and appointed officials to rule them.

In other ways, this great Carolingian ruler acted, throughout his reign, as if he, rather than the Pope, were head of the Church. He legislated for the clergy within his domains in capitularies that made no mention of papal authority. In 794 it was he, and not the Roman pontiff, who called together a great Church council that dealt with the religious problems caused by the Adoptionist heresy in Christian Spain, which was a revival of Arian ideas there, and by Iconoclasm in the Byzantine Empire. Against the Pope's wishes, he decided that Empress Irene's repudiation of Iconoclasm in 787 did not mark the end of the schism between the Eastern and Western Churches. Even the Pope's presumption in crowning him Emperor in 800 annoyed him, according to his biographer, Einhard. Although his successor, Louis, showed more regard for papal sensibilities, he too made sure that the control of the Church remained in Imperial hands. On his own initiative, he convened a second reforming council at Aix-la-Chapelle in 816, and continued to legislate for the Church in capitularies, much as his father had done. The Carolingian era, in sum, was one in which Caesaropapism became the rule in the Western Church, and in which the Papacy, although respected, therefore played a minor role.

THE CHURCH IN THE EAST

Charles the Great was no doubt determined to exercise no lesser powers than had his predecessors and rivals in Constantinople, for the Byzantine emperors maintained almost complete control over the Church during this era. It was Leo who, on his own initiative, promulgated the decrees that proclaimed Iconoclasm, while his son, Constantine V, did not hesitate to remove from office patriarchs and other high Church officials. He even called together Church conclaves that were completely uncanonical, to implement an extreme Iconoclast program. When Irene determined to end this heresy, she did so on her own initiative as empress, although she was wise enough to call together a canonical Church council to give assent to her actions. A little while later, when Iconoclasm was revived, its restoration was the work of emperors who imposed their views on a somewhat reluctant Church. Seldom in the history of the Church had there been a period in which Caesaropapism was as unrestrained as it was in the Byzantium of this period.

On the other hand, the Eastern Church lagged behind the Western in the conversion of pagan peoples. Just as it had earlier, it showed little interest in spreading Christianity beyond the Empire's borders, perhaps because the struggle over Iconoclasm engaged its full energies. Thus it allowed the Slavs and the Bulgars to remain pagan, and made little effort to spread Christianity among the Kazars, whose upper classes remained attached to Judaism.

Furthermore, these years saw a crisis for monasticism

in the Greek Church, in contrast to its flourishing state in the Latin West. During the reign of Constantine V, Imperial policy turned against monasticism. This was because the monasteries were centers of anti-Iconoclast sentiment and their vast estates made them obstacles to the peasants' military tenures so favored by the early Isaurian emperors; moreover, these soldier-emperors tended to regard monks as drones who refused to aid in the defense of the Empire from outside attack. The result was persecution of monks, confiscation of monastic lands, and the closing of abbeys throughout the Empire. Although monasticism returned to favor under Irene, her Iconoclast successors renewed pressures against monastic establishments. By 840, the result was an Eastern monasticism that had been much weakened and was to recover its strength only slowly in the decades ahead.

Cultural Life

THE CAROLINGIAN EMPIRE

By the beginning of the eighth century, the cultural life of Europe, especially in the West, had sunk to a level as low as that which it had reached during the late fifth century. The Moorish conquest of Spain had brought to an end the late Roman secular culture of the Iberian Peninsula, which had long remained vigorous, while in Merovingian Gaul during the same period decadence was widespread. The courts of the early Carolingian Mayors of the Palace, Charles Martel and Pepin, seem like pale copies of those of their Merovingian predecessors, and their charters, written in a barbarous Latin, are a witness to the decline of learning. Charlemagne himself grew to manhood unable to read or write. In only a few northern French monasteries, where Anglo-Saxon influence was strong, was any cultural tradition preserved—and at that, in a form that was narrower than that of earlier Merovingian times.

If there was any real cultural vigor in the West, it was apparently to be found only in the British Isles and in the Lombard kingdom of Italy. Yet when we examine the actual situation in the British Isles, the result is somewhat disappointing. Though Irish abbeys continued to be centers of study, they now lacked the ability to break new ground for the intellect. As for Britain, the vigorous intellectual activity that had helped produce Bede slowed down after his death, even though Alcuin and other Anglo-Saxons were to provide most of the intellectual life at the Carolingian court, and to write much of the rather stilted poetry that was produced in court circles. But while Alcuin showed that something of value could still be found in the Northumbrian tradition, he represented almost the last flowering of the Anglo-Saxon monastic mind for many decades.

In Lombard Italy, where some prosperity existed, there was more intellectual life. At Pavia, down to 774, such kings as Luidprand continued to codify and add to Lombard law. They also maintained at their court a tradition of patronage of late Roman secular learning, and were concerned with preserving the historical traditions of their people. They supported monasteries in which scribes were active and to which Visigothic scholars fled with their books. It must be admitted, however, that even this Italy of the Lombards, along with nearby papal Rome, seems civilized only by comparison with the lack of culture in most of the rest of western Europe.

A change came with the reign of Charlemagne. As this great Carolingian ruler completed the work of his predecessors and began to see himself as the equal of the emperor of Constantinople, he gave increasing attention to the cultural level of his lands. Perhaps it was his own deficiencies that spurred him on, or else he saw the need for a more educated clergy; for heresy and ignorance, in his view, went hand in hand. Perhaps his contacts with more advanced Byzantine areas, after his conquests in Lombardy and Visigothic Spain, made him understand better the need for giving a broader scope to his Empire. Certainly the role he assigned himself in the Church required a better-schooled clergy. The outcome was what has often been called—not without exaggeration—the Carolingian Renaissance.

The center of the revival was Charlemagne's court at Aix-la-Chapelle, to which he attracted scholars from all over western Europe: Alcuin from England, Dicuil from Ireland, Peter of Pisa, and Paul the Deacon from Italy, as well as a number of Visigothic men of letters and some talented men who were available in his own Frankish heartland. He established a palace school to educate his own children and those of his principal nobles, and reorganized his chancery. Soon his efforts spread more widely. Throughout the later years of his reign, he made a conscious effort to improve the education of his clergy, especially that which was available in monastic institutions. He ordered every abbey to keep annals and establish schools, and he encouraged standardization of the script, using that of Tours as a model. His plan was to have clerical education extended to the entire lay population.

The culture that resulted was in some ways undistinguished, perhaps because those who were mainly engaged in it were almost all churchmen. Yet in comparison with what had immediately preceded it, this was a remarkable accomplishment. It resulted in a renewed interest in classical Latin authors, whose manuscripts were now prized, and whose style influenced that of Alcuin and Lupus of Ferrières. It stimulated the writing of an original Latin poetry, most of it religious. It led to the writing of history and biography, as seen in Einhard's *Life of Charlemagne*, Paul the Deacon's *History of the Lombards*, as well as of numerous monastic annals, some of which, like the *Royal Annals*, approached contemporary history. It produced a chancery that could compose charters and capitularies in a clear vigorous Latin style. It issued codes of law for those peoples of the Empire whose law had not as yet been written down. Finally, it encouraged the revival of Church music, especially choral chant.

The revival did not come to an end with Charlemagne. On the contrary, it proved powerful enough to transmit a certain tradition of learning to churchmen and laymen of the following generation. During the reign of Louis the Pious, we find a Thegan or an Astronomus writing imperial biographies, and an Ermold composing a long narrative poem in the emperor's honor. This revival even began, after a lapse of several centuries, to stimulate interest in philosophical ideas of a narrow religious sort, in the writings of Gottschalk and Raban Maur. Both at the Carolingian court and in monastic and cathedral schools, a limited but broadly based western European intellectual tradition had appeared by 840; it stressed Latin literature and poetry, history and biography, law and administration, and some theological speculation. Moreover, this culture soon began to influence Anglo-Saxon England and the northwestern Spanish kingdoms on the other side of the Pyrenees.

THE BYZANTINE EMPIRE

By contrast with the cultural revival in the West during the late Carolingian period, the intellectual life of the Byzantine Empire was stagnant down to 800, despite the fact that a considerable body of educated laymen continued to exist here, and the level of economic life was considerably higher than in western Europe. Perhaps this cultural stagnation was due in part to the stultifying effects of the Iconoclast controversy, which occupied the better minds of the age in Byzantium to the exclusion of anything else. Perhaps it was because the campaigns against monasticism by the Isaurian emperors left monastic circles culturally impoverished. Only in the field of law do we glimpse much intellectual vigor within the Empire. The composition of the Isaurian code of laws called the *Ecloga* shows a Byzantine ability to develop Christian principles of jurisprudence that were different from those found in the Justinian Code. On the other hand, we have no evidence that any histories were composed during this troubled eighth century; not until the ninth were they resumed. And the most subtle theological speculation in the East was written by John of Damascus, who lived in Moslem territory beyond the boundaries of the Empire.

What is true of the intellectual life of Byzantium is even truer of its art and architecture. This soldier-dominated age did little building except for military fortifications. In the field of art, of course, the Iconoclast movement paralyzed creativity, since its opposition to the use of religious images halted the development of mosaic art and icons, which had been the glory of Byzantium in previous periods. It is possible that some revival of classical secular artistic traditions did take place, as seen from the discovery of a few fragments of mosaics from the Imperial palace at Constantinople; but if so, it did not, as yet, have much impact on the artists of the time. Only at St. Catherine's monastery in Sinai, far from Constantinople, is there evidence of a continuing artistic tradition that linked this age with that which preceded it and that which was to follow.

THE ARTS IN THE WEST

Western Europe, on the other hand, shows more evidence of architectural and artistic development. Although the churches in Rome that date from this period are disappointing, both in their architecture and in their decoration, which seem crude and repetitive of older Romano-Byzantine themes, in Lombardy we find a new vigor. Here, in a number of churches, the architects of the period developed a new technique of supporting the stone roofs of their buildings by a system of ribbed cross-vaults which carried the thrust of their weight—an innovation that was to make possible the vaulting of later Romanesque and Gothic cathedrals. Elsewhere in the Empire, however, there is little evidence of architectural innovation. The churches that date from these years are small, simple structures; when Charlemagne built his chapel at Aix-la-Chapelle, he characteristically copied buildings that had been constructed earlier at Ravenna.

On the other hand, Carolingian art, as seen in manuscript illumination, reveals a real synthesis of surviving artistic traditions, similar to that which was taking place in intellectual life. Classical, Byzantine, barbarian, and Anglo-Saxon motifs are blended together in a new way, and a certain naturalism added to them to produce for the first time—in the Utrecht Psalter, for instance—a distinctively western European art style. The same tendency is revealed in the surviving church frescos and in such minor forms as ivories and chalices. This distinctive Carolingian art did not, however, replace older artistic styles in northern Europe. Irish and Anglo-Saxon manuscripts, such as the *Book of Kells*, reveal the colorful imagination of earlier Celtic art, as do Celtic crosses and jewelry.

In distant Scandinavia, far from the Carolingian world, we find a vigorous native artistic tradition persisting. Here, in the beautiful silver jewelry from Gotland that has survived since that age, and in objects buried in the Gokstad and Oseberg ships, we see that artistic traditions derived from earlier Nordic art were still alive and vigorous. The beautiful, delicate interlaced carvings on Queen Asa's yacht seem particularly significant in this respect.

Thus Europe, during the eighth and early ninth centuries, preserved artistic traditions of earlier times: barbarian German, Celtic, classical, and Byzantine. In the Carolingian Empire, these styles began to fuse to form an art that we can think of as distinctly Western; in Lombardy, a new architecture was being born. While preserving much of the heritage of their Roman and barbarian past, the peoples of Europe were at last beginning to lay the foundation of a more varied and distinctive civilization.

chapter IV

The Age of
the Vikings, A.D. 840–911

T he seven decades that follow the death of Louis the Pious in 840 mark a period of great change in Europe, in some ways resembling that of the barbarian invasions. When they were over, the Carolingian Empire had disintegrated, and a new nexus had appeared in northern Europe, from the British Isles to Kiev—one that owed its existence to the peoples of Scandinavia. These Scandinavians left their homes in large numbers to raid the shores of western Europe, and to settle areas in the Atlantic as far west as Greenland. At the same time, others, joined by some Baltic peoples, traversed the Baltic, penetrated deep into Russia, and even raided the southern shores of the Black Sea and the Caspian.

Although these Viking and Varangian Scandinavians were chiefly responsible for the changes that took place during these years, they were not the only peoples whose impact helped to produce a new Europe. From Spain and North Africa, Moslem seamen set forth to capture the islands of the Mediterranean from Byzantium, and to raid the shores of Christian Europe. From both the north and the south, the more organized parts of Europe found themselves under attack, by enemies whose command of the sea made it difficult to resist them with any degree of success. Finally, at the end of the period, a nomadic people, the Magyars, advanced from south Russia, occupied the Hungarian plain, and began to raid southern Germany and northern Italy, thus adding to Europe's distress.

An Age of Invasions

SCANDINAVIAN MOVEMENTS

The Scandinavian movements to the west and south, which affected so much of Europe, were made possible, as has been noted, by the development of superior ships. They were perhaps touched off by Charlemagne's attacks on Denmark, which drove the Danes to reply with naval assaults of their own upon the coasts of the Carolingian Empire. Perhaps Scandinavian overpopulation in certain regions of the north had a role to play too. Soon, however, such attacks, which had proven very profitable to the original participants, helped to produce a pirate mentality throughout Scandinavia; many others now joined in to acquire booty and plunder for themselves as well along the shores of western Europe. And as such attacks escalated, they began to assume certain patterns, which affected each part of Europe a little differently.

Although a few Norwegian and Danish pirates had

raided the shores of the British Isles and the Carolingian Empire before the death of Charlemagne, their first permanent conquests came during the 820s and 830s. During these decades, bands of Norwegians, led by chiefs related to the royal family of the Westfold near Oslo, established themselves in Ireland, with Dublin as their capital, and settled in the Hebrides and Westmoreland as well. For the next few decades, they confined their activities to raids; in about 870, they began to settle the more distant Faroes and Iceland. This latter island attracted numerous settlers, some of whom even ventured as far west as Greenland during the course of the tenth century.

Meanwhile other Vikings, mainly Danish, were raiding the shores of the North Sea, where, about 840, they established themselves permanently in Frisia. From Frisia, they went on to raid the coasts and the interior of the western regions of the Carolingian Empire for more than two decades. In 865, a large army of these freebooters invaded England, determined to conquer it. But Alfred the Great defeated them and, in 878, forced them to make peace; this still left in their possession, however, a large part of eastern England, known as the Danelaw. Soon after this defeat, these Vikings began to lose some of their conquests. They were expelled from Frisia, while Alfred and his son Edward forced them out of London and some of their strongholds in the Midlands. Then in 911, when their power was waning, they were able to establish themselves near the mouth of the Seine in a region granted their leader, Rollo, by King Charles the Simple of France—a territory soon known as Normandy.

Equally interesting is the story of Scandinavian expansion toward the east. During the late eighth and early ninth centuries, a number of Scandinavians, mainly Swedish, who were joined by other peoples from the Baltic area and were known collectively as Varangians, moved into northern Russia, where they found a number of trading centers, including Novgorod, Old Ladoga, and Smolensk, already in existence. Some of them traveled down the Volga to the land of the Kazars and even to the Islamic world of the Middle East. For a brief period toward the middle of the ninth century, when the Varangians were expelled from Russia, such contacts were interrupted.

Between 850 and 860, however, according to the late and perhaps legendary account in the *Russian Primary Chronicle*, the Varangians were invited to return. Two of their leaders, Askold and Dir, reached Kiev, where they gathered an armed force strong enough to proceed south by way of the Dnieper and the Black Sea and, in 860–861, to attack Constantinople. A little while later, another Scandinavian adventurer, named Rurik, who was perhaps a Dane, made himself ruler of Novgorod. He was succeeded by a certain Oleg, who, a few years later, mustered a large native Russian force and advanced south to conquer Kiev. By the 880s Oleg had achieved sufficient success in war to be able to unite the various cities and districts of northern and central Russia, and to form a Kievan principality.

Oleg and his immediate successors, however, were interested in more than the establishment of such a Russian state; they also desired to open up trade routes. Hence they sent expeditions down the Volga to break the power of the White Bulgars and the Kazars, who had previously monopolized trade along this river. In 907, they sent another force south by way of the Dnieper; they attacked the Byzantine Empire again and produced the famous trade treaty of 911 between Byzantium and Rus merchants. Finally, they sent expeditions to the southwest; these, combined with

Pechenek pressure, helped to drive the Magyars into Hungary, and opened up a trade route north of the Carpathians to southeastern Germany by way of Cracow and Prague. By 907, this had resulted in the appearance of Russian merchants at Raffelstein on the upper Danube. By the early tenth century, a new Russian state had appeared, in some measure as the result of Scandinavian efforts; this new state controlled the trade routes that led to southern Germany, Byzantium, and the Moslem Middle East.

The great movement of the Scandinavian peoples, which led to the foundation of principalities from Russia to Ireland, Normandy, and the English Danelaw, by virtue of the fact that it drew off surplus and unruly elements also helped to advance political consolidation in Scandinavia itself. A Danish kingdom already existed. Now another arose in Norway, the creation of Harold Fairhair, a local kinglet of the Oslo region, who conquered the jarls or chieftains of Norway's west coast, to form a Norwegian state. According to Norse tradition, his conquest helped to drive a number of independent-minded chiefs westward to colonize Iceland. At about the same time, Swedish kings of the Uppsala region also began to dominate a wider area of Sweden, and one of them, named Gnupa, advanced south to seize Hedeby in the Jutland peninsula, an important gateway to the trade of the North Sea. By the early tenth century, Scandinavia, organized into three distinct kingdoms, was playing a part in the political history of Europe.

MOSLEM SEAFARING

As Scandinavians began to make their influence felt over much of northern Europe, Moslem seafarers from

Spain and North Africa did the same thing on the Mediterranean side. They were given their opportunity by the decline of Carolingian seapower, which had always been slight in the area, and by the fatal weakening of Byzantine fleets during the last troubled years of Iconoclasm. In 826–827, a group of Moslem freebooters, originally Spanish, who had been expelled from Alexandria after holding it for a decade, sailed across the Mediterranean and seized the island of Crete from the Byzantines. A year or so later, North African Moslems began to attack and to occupy Sicily. The struggle was a long and hard one, for Byzantium made a valiant effort to hold the island. By 902, however, all of the island and nearby Malta as well were in Moslem hands, and Moslem naval strength had so increased that it had also neutralized Corsica and Sardinia. At about the same period, Spanish Moslems, after reorganizing their fleet, which had suffered at the hands of Viking raiders, occupied the Balearics.

While these islands of the Mediterranean were being seized, bands of Moslem adventurers were advancing north, to found small pirate bases on the shores of the European mainland. The most important of them were Fraxinetum in Provence, Monte Garigliano near Naples, Bari at the entrance to the Adriatic, and a base near Athens, along the shores of the Attic peninsula. Some of these advanced bases did not long endure. Bari was retaken by a joint Carolingian-Venetian-Byzantine expedition soon after 870, and the Attic base was probably wiped out at about the same time, while Monte Garigliano was reconquered in 916. The pattern that had developed by 911, however, seems clear. The Mediterranean had become a Moslem lake: only Venice, at the head of the Adriatic, and Constantinople, on the Bosphorus, were capable of disputing Moslem mastery of the Mediterranean on a local basis. Byzantine control of the Mediterranean, which had been so significant in Isaurian times, had given way to Moslem domination of the Middle Sea.

Political Repercussions

ON THE WEST

The organized states of Europe all felt the impact of the Moslem and Scandinavian invaders. Even the emirate of Cordova was weakened rather than strengthened by Moslem expansion in the Mediterranean: although it continued to be nominally ruled by Ommayad successors of Abd-ar-Rahman I, it was filled with disorder. Revolts were constant, not only among Moslem factions, but also among the Christian population, some of whom, in cities like Cordova, dramatized their opposition to Islam by proselytizing openly and seeking martyrdom. The Moslem border lords of the Ebro valley ignored Cordova and achieved a *de facto* independence, while the Christian rulers of Asturias advanced south of the Douro line. Even in Catalonia, a powerful local prince, Count Wilfred, began to occupy the deserted plain of Ausona. By the first years of the tenth century, it looked doubtful whether this last great conquest of Islam in the West would hold together as an organized state.

In the Carolingian Empire, the situation was even worse. The death of Louis the Pious saw the Empire divided into three portions: West Francia, ruled by Charles the Bald; the East Frankish kingdom, ruled by Lewis; and a central region, which stretched from the North Sea to Rome, and was controlled by Lothaire, who bore the Imperial title. Almost at once Lotharingia lost any unity it might have possessed. It was divided into Lorraine, Provence, and Italy, while some of its northern borderlands were gobbled up by the French and German Carolingian kings. When this happened, the West Frankish kingdom of Charles disintegrated, too. Constant wars between Charles and his nephew Pepin, punctuated by revolts of the magnates and Viking attacks, proved its undoing. In 887, a decade after Charles' death, it fell into the hands of a king who had been chosen from a rival noble family.

By 911, both the West Frankish lands and Lotharingia had lost all political cohesion. The former, now again ruled by a Carolingian monarch, Charles the Simple, hardly existed as a viable political entity, for its king had no authority south of the Loire and little authority north of it. Lotharingia was in worse shape. Its northern portion was now as feudalized as northern France, while in Provence and Italy nominal kings had lost control over a nobility who ignored all efforts to control them.

The East Frankish or German kingdom followed a somewhat different course of development. Less exposed to Viking attack than other areas of the Empire, it remained strong under Lewis the German and Arnulf. Until the end of the ninth century, it kept its Carolingian administrative system relatively intact, was able to defeat those Norsemen who attacked it, and advanced its authority into Central Europe, where many Slavs accepted its hegemony. Not until the death of Arnulf and the reign of his infant son, Lewis, did it begin to lose cohesion. Then it, too, disintegrated into a number of *stem* duchies, which seem to have been organized on a proto-tribal basis, and began to suffer from attacks by the Magyars, who were now established in Hungary. By 911, it had sunk into a weakness from which it was not to recover until the second half of the tenth century.

In the British Isles, on the other hand, the invasions stimulated a strong reaction. In Ireland, it is true, the establishment of the Norse kingdom of Dublin kept the Irish tribes of the interior from developing an effective government of their own. But in Britain, after the Danes had failed in their attempt to conquer the entire country, Alfred the Great and his son Edward proceeded with a slow reconquest of parts of the Danelaw, and new territory was added, as far as Chester. Gradually a new English state, with institutions that were unique in the Europe of that time, began to emerge. A similar process of consolidation took place in the north. We do not know exactly how this came about, but perhaps the Scots of Dalraida, the Britons of Strathclyde, the Angles of Bernecia, and the Picts of eastern Scotland hoped to find strength in a union under a new royal house. Scotland, like Alfred's England, had not yet assumed a truly national form, but we can see at least the outlines of it appearing.

Similar changes took place in parts of Central Europe, where a Greater Moravia had emerged by 840. Its rulers, Moimir, Radislav, and Sviatopolk, resisted the pressures of the East Frankish Carolingians, and spread their domain over much of the central Danube valley. They established diplomatic relations with Constantinople and welcomed missionaries from there. Although the Magyars shattered their state, enough of it remained to form the nucleus of a strong Bohemia, which was to emerge during the course of the tenth century.

Even more important was Bulgaria, which had now become Slavicized, and had extended its borders to become a Bulgarian Empire. It was ruled by able monarchs, who kept a steady pressure on Byzantium, while borrowing from the latter both political institutions and much of its superior civilization. Nor did its rulers fail to see the advantages to be gained from entering into close relations with both the Papacy and the rulers of Germany, as they expanded their Empire. By 911, they had become formidable rivals of the Byzantine Empire.

IN BYZANTIUM

Byzantium, unlike the Carolingian Empire in the West, managed not only to survive its difficulties, but even to emerge stronger than ever, despite the attacks of the Varangian Rus, the Bulgars, and the Arabs. There were several reasons for its success. In the first place, the Empire found an able ruler in Basil I, the founder of a new Macedonian dynasty. Secondly, by 843 Iconoclasm was played out, and a new orthodoxy emerged; accepted by the entire Empire, it restored religious unity to a divided Byzantine world. Thanks to all this, although it lost Sicily to the Moslems, Byzantium was able to reestablish its authority in southern Italy, most of the Illyrian coast, and much of central Greece. Despite its failure to prevent the Bulgarians from dominating much of the Balkans, by the early tenth century a Byzantine Empire had emerged, which had weathered the storms of the ninth century and was ready to enjoy a new period of strength.

If the Viking age saw the Carolingian Empire disintegrate, this decline was more than offset by growing political cohesion elsewhere. Not only were national states emerging in Scandinavia, but Viking pressures led to the beginnings of a national England and a national Scotland as well. Scandinavian adventurers played an important part in the emergence of Kievan Russia, as a result of which Kazar control over the south Russian steppes was weakened; in Central Europe, therefore, two Slavic states took shape: Greater Moravia and the Bulgarian Empire. Only north of the Carpathians was there a region that still lacked an advanced political system of its own. Now most of the continent had reached a certain degree of cohesion; the age of tribal Europe had almost ended.

Social and Economic Impact

ON TRADE

The impact of the invasions on European economic life was similar. On the one hand, the settled and economically advanced areas of Europe suffered serious damage at the hands of Viking, Moslem, and Hungarian raiders; one needs only to read the monkish chronicles of the time to see a picture of destruction, death, and pillage. On the other hand, the activities of these raiders, especially those of the Vikings, also brought specific advantages to certain parts of Europe.

In the first place, thanks to Scandinavian expansion, much of the northwestern European economic area of Carolingian times, which faced the northern seas, came to be firmly linked to the Russian-Kazarian region and became in effect part of a single large trading area, extending from Ireland, England, and the Low Countries to the Black and Caspian seas. As a result of Kiev's new trade treaty with Byzantium, this trading area was now directly connected with the gold-rich Byzantine world as well. This is shown by the coin hoards dating from this period. They reveal that Moslem silver dirhems, long the dominant coinage of Russia and the Baltic, had reached Germany, Flanders, and Britain by the early tenth century, while German and English silver money had spread east during that same time, to reach Sweden and Finland.

Trade along northern European trade routes resulted in an exchange of western European wine, wheat, woolens, weapons, and metalware for furs, slaves, silks, spices, and silver. Some of these latter products were in turn obtained from Byzantium and the Islamic Middle East via Russia, in return for slaves, furs, honey, beeswax, and swords. In the western portion of this great trading area, Frisian, Anglo-Saxon, Scandinavian, Jewish, and German merchants were active, while in the eastern part of it, Slavic, Scandinavian, Kazar, and Moslem merchants played the dominant role. The Scandinavian element knit the whole region together economically, as it did politically: it was in the Baltic that eastern and western trade currents met and mingled.

By the end of this period, a somewhat similar situation had developed in the Mediterranean. Here Moslem conquest of such islands as Sicily and Malta linked parts of Spain and North Africa with Syria and Egypt —regions that had enjoyed commercial intercourse only intermittently since the late seventh century. It is true that commerce developed slowly along these Mediterranean routes; by 911, Venice and Naples were the only ports in western Europe that seem to have had merchants who were enterprising enough to trade with Moslem Africa. All in all, then, this trading area was much less important, as far as Europe was concerned, than that which had developed in the north.

Northeast of this Mediterranean Moslem-dominated

trading area lay that of Byzantium. It was somewhat smaller than it had been earlier; but it still included Asia Minor, the Black Sea, the Balkan coasts, and most of Italy, where its gold nomisma coinage circulated freely. Its new direct commerce with Kiev supplemented older links with Kazaria, and an expanded trade now reached central Europe by way of Saloniki. This probably compensated for the decrease in the volume of traffic that reached Italian ports, since such commerce was limited by Moslem piracy from Crete and Sicily.

On the whole, Byzantium's role as a middleman and major supplier of luxury goods to western Europe did not change much during these years. Furthermore, it was still primarily by way of northern Italy that northwestern Europe traded with Byzantium and the Moslems of the Mediterranean. From Venice and the Po valley, a considerable amount of commerce continued to cross the Alps to the Rhinelands and the North Sea. Along this route, Jews were now settled in considerable numbers as merchant intermediaries.

On the other hand, most of France, northwestern Spain, and northwestern Italy were increasingly isolated from the trade currents of the period. This was in contrast to the situation in Carolingian times and can be accounted for by Moslem piracy and in part, perhaps, by Viking attacks. In any event, local trade now became the rule in this part of Europe. A few Jews still carried slaves through Septimania to Spain and exchanged them there for luxury wares. A few northern French traders crossed Alpine passes to seek goods in northern Italy. There was also some trade of a local form from northern France to Ireland, England, and the Low Countries. But all of this trade was on a very small scale.

Central Europe suffered similar economic isolation.

After a brief period in the ninth century, when goods traveled relatively freely along the middle Danube trade routes, the incursion of the Magyars into the Hungarian plain put an end to such traffic for some decades. There is evidence, just prior to 911, of trade passing by land north of the Carpathians to Kiev, but this traffic did not become important until later in the tenth century.

The overall picture of European economic development thus indicates that most trading places in the western part of the Carolingian Empire declined steadily, while some of them, along the Mediterranean shores between Barcelona and the Tiber, all but disappeared. The number of mints that remained in operation in the same area also declined. In southern France, for example, by the early tenth century only Toulouse, Melle, Lepuy, Clermont, Vienne, and Arles still coined money; a similar, although less drastic, diminution took place in northern France. On the other hand, trading places in Ireland, such as Dublin, flourished and, by the early tenth century, the same thing was true of much of England. In the Low Countries, Viking attacks affected a number of centers, but most of them continued to be active, especially those that traded with Scandinavia.

In Germany, there was even more economic activity. Here Rhineland centers attracted a new population, and new trading places appeared between the Elbe and the Rhine, to join in the commerce that was reaching the North Sea and Baltic. In southern Germany, others grew in importance, in response to the trade that was crossing the Alps from Italy. In the Baltic region, trading centers also increased in importance during this period; these included Hedeby, at the base of the Jutland peninsula; Birka, near the entrance to the Malar Sea in Sweden; and Apoloné and Seeburg, on the eastern shores of the Baltic. Such Russian towns as Nov-

gorod, Ladoga, Smolensk, Kiev, and Chernikov, stimulated by traffic with Constantinople and the Moslem
East, also grew considerably.

In Italy, Naples, which traded both with Byzantium
and with the nearby Moslems of Sicily and North
Africa, remained a city of importance. So did Venice,
whose favorable location allowed it to export timber and
slaves and metal products that had been obtained in
Germany and Central Europe, and to import Moslem
and Byzantine wares. Such traffic was already helping
to provide this city with a considerable fleet, which
could be used to dominate nearby Dalmatian coasts and
to clear Moslem pirates from Bari at the entrance to
the Adriatic. Venice's prosperity was shared, in part,
by other north Italian cities in the Po valley, such as
Milan and Pavia, which were beginning to be visited
by English and German merchants who were seeking
Eastern wares.

Constantinople, the metropolis of the Byzantine Empire, continued to be Europe's most important city
during these years. As a trading center, it was visited by
Moslem, Italian, Jewish, and Russian merchants; it was
an important manufacturing center as well, in which,
according to *The Book of the Prefect*, silks and other
luxury wares were produced for international markets.
These years of Viking and Moslem attack thus saw a
considerable growth in Europe's overall commerce,
which probably more than offset the decline that was
apparent in France, northwestern Spain, and parts of
northwest Italy.

ON AGRICULTURE

In agriculture, there was a similar differentiation. If
Viking attacks bore particularly heavily upon the

peasantry in the British Isles and France, who could not protect themselves, in those parts of Europe that were not exposed to outside attacks, a good deal of the progress that had been made in Carolingian times continued. In France, Britain, and Provence, and in some Alpine regions, where pirate bases were established, rural areas were so disorganized that in some cases cultivation of the soil had altogether ceased. On the other hand, in northwest Spain, land between the Douro and the Cantabrian mountains continued to attract new settlers, as did the deserted plain of Ausona in Catalonia. In Auvergne in central France, considerable clearing of the waste took place, and in Germany too, prior to Magyar attacks, much new land was put into cultivation, especially in Westphalia and along the upper Danube, as well as in Slavic areas just north of the Carpathians.

There is less evidence of agricultural progress in other parts of Europe, except for areas such as Lombardy, which were shielded from outside attack, and parts of Greece and Macedonia, which benefited from better Byzantine defenses. But an overall view of European agriculture seems to show a continued effort to put new land into cultivation, and an increase in the continent's food supply, despite invasion and disorder.

THE SEIGNEURIAL SYSTEM

One result of these years of invasion in Europe was a steady increase in the number of fortifications that were built. Alfred and Edward the Elder had fortified boroughs built to protect their kingdom from Danish attacks; in northern and western France, the answer to the invasions was the castle. Moslem assaults on southern French coasts also stimulated castle construction near the mouths of the Rhone; Count Wilfred built a number of them to assist his colonization of Ausona. In northern Italy, too, there was considerable castle construction during these years.

Wherever such castles appeared, they tended to increase the power of a fighting upper class of warriors who alone, as large landowners, could afford the expense of their construction and the equipment needed for war. Thus this aristocracy became an even more militarized class than had been the case in Carolingian times. Even in Germany, which was backward by comparison with West Frankish lands, Arnulf relied upon such a class to furnish the cavalry with which he opposed the Danes in 892 at the Battle of the Dyle.

This was true also in Byzantium, where large landowners furnished the heavily armed cavalry forces that Basil I used in southern Italy and to oppose the Bulgarians. Everywhere the trend toward aristocratic control over the peasantry—an essentially seigneurial system—was accentuated. Sometimes, where the government had broken down, as was the case in the West Frankish kingdom, the result was a feudalized social structure. Elsewhere, in England, Germany, or Byzantium, where government remained effective, the tendency toward feudalization was checked. Everywhere, however, the freeborn peasant or small proprietor lost much of the independence he had earlier possessed.

THE CHURCH

The disorders of this age of invasions seriously affected the Church. Western monasticism, which had been so important to the Church in Carolingian times, perhaps suffered most. Since the Vikings, Moslems, and

Magyars were all pagans, they had no compunction about attacking monasteries; on the other hand, since abbeys were unfortified and located in rural areas, they could not be protected. Thus by 911 many of them had been sacked, sometimes repeatedly. In areas such as Gascony, Provence, and parts of the British Isles, this resulted in the disappearance of monasticism. In other regions, such as southern Italy and the area about Rome, the result was an insecurity that adversely affected monastic growth and vitality. This decline, however, was not completely due to outside invasions. Local magnates were not averse, in these unsettled times, to taking over monastic property for their own private use. The case of Count Baldwin of Flanders, who seized land that belonged to the abbeys of his county, was only one example of a process that was being repeated, over and over again, in many parts of western Europe. When Alfred the Great decided to encourage monasticism in his realm in the late ninth century, he found that he had to rebuild the abbeys almost from scratch.

There were, however, areas in which monasticism held its own, and even grew in importance. This was true of Catalonia and parts of northwest Spain, as well as of areas in central and northern France and Germany, where the Carolingian impetus continued during this age of invasions. It was also true of the Po valley.

If monasticism suffered severely in certain areas, it withstood the crisis better than did the Western Church's secular hierarchy and organization. At first the Church, within the Carolingian Empire, was strengthened as the Imperial authority declined. Charlemagne's successors, however, were unable to maintain the powers he had been able to exercise over the

Church, and the episcopacy emerged as the undisputed champion of a Western Christian Empire. It was Archbishop Hincmar who reminded later Carolingian monarchs of their Imperial responsibilities, while the Popes again assumed a role that had been impossible only a few decades earlier. This explains the career of Pope Nicholas I, perhaps the most outstanding pontiff after Gregory the Great. Nicholas used the pseudo-Isidorean *Decretals* to assert his authority over prelates like Hincmar, and he admonished such monarchs as Lothaire of Lorraine. He employed diplomatic means in attempting to bring Bulgaria under papal authority, and put pressure upon Byzantine emperors, who were seeking to end the schism with Rome, to dismiss Photius, the Patriarch of Constantinople.

But the independence and authority enjoyed by the Popes and the secular hierarchy did not long endure. As conditions worsened and disorders increased in the West, churchmen found that they had escaped from Carolingian Caesaropapism only to fall under the more brutal domination of those families who controlled the regions where their sees were located. By the tenth century, such families had taken over Church offices as a private right and had made them an adjunct of family power. A feudalized Church appeared as a result, and even the Papacy became the creature of quarreling noble families in Rome. Having lost both the protection of the Carolingians and the independence it had enjoyed at the time of Hincmar and Nicholas I, it was a weaker Church that emerged in the West by the early tenth century.

These facts help explain why the Western Church was no longer a very effective agent in spreading Christianity among the pagan peoples of Europe. St. Anskar could still travel to Uppsala to convert the Swedes; Al-

fred could still force King Guthram and his Danes, settled in the Danelaw, to accept baptism as a price of
peace; a few German missionaries could still try to
spread Christianity among the Slavs of the middle
Danube region. But little was accomplished by such
efforts, for the Western Church, plundered by invaders and enslaved by its own fighting aristocracy, was a
much less effective organization than it had been in
earlier centuries.

The Greek Church, paradoxically, was in much better shape. In the first place, the end of Iconoclasm and
the collapse of the rival Carolingian Empire removed
the basic causes of the schism with the Latin West.
Under Michael III and Basil I, relations were renewed
with the Papacy. There were ensuing difficulties, for
an element within the Greek Church, led by Photius,
opposed this enterprise, and the Papacy too proved in-
tractable on occasion. But the Byzantine emperors
persisted, and were even willing at times to force their
own Church into line, until, by the end of the century,
the schism finally ended. No doubt the revival of Byzantine authority in southern Italy, after the dispatch
of armies there, helped bring about this rapproche-
ment, for the Popes, who could no longer count on
Carolingians to protect Rome from the Moslems, found
it wiser to accommodate themselves to Byzantine rulers
who would. At any rate, by 911 Byzantine Imperial influence in Rome was greater than it had been at any
time since Iconoclasm.

The ending of the schism, however, did not mean
that the emperors in Constantinople were willing to
modify Caesaropapism, as far as their own Eastern
Church was concerned. Basil I and Leo the Wise
showed this clearly. Although no emperor after the
end of Iconoclasm in 843 meddled with doctrine, all

made it clear that they were masters of their Church
and expected to be obeyed by the hierarchy. And
while they were willing to accommodate themselves to
papal authority in Italy and western Europe, they opposed its extension into the Balkans, where Serbs and
Bulgarians were adopting Christianity during these
years. They were in the end successful in these efforts,
and, by the early tenth century, the Eastern Church was
under firm Imperial control, a fact that the Papacy
was tacitly willing to recognize.

Another important development was the revival of
monasticism. The monasteries had been resolute opponents of Iconoclasm, and the ending of the heresy
made them the principal beneficiaries of the change.
Favored by the emperors of the Macedonian line, who
endowed them generously with land and privileges,
monasteries again began to play an important role in
the Eastern Church, especially in the European and
Aegean provinces of the Empire.

Moreover, at a time when monasticism seemed to
be declining in the West, the revitalized monasticism
of the Byzantine Empire played an important part in
the new missionary effort that the Eastern Church now
initiated beyond the Imperial borders. It began when
two monks, Cyril and Methodius, left the Saloniki region to bring Christianity to the Slavs of Greater Moravia. Realizing that their efforts would be more effective
if their converts understood them better, they trans-
lated the Scriptures into Slavic so as to assist their missionary effort. They, and others who followed them,
were encouraged in their efforts by the Byzantine emperors, who saw in such activity a way of checking
Frankish and papal influence in Central Europe and
the Balkans, especially in Bulgaria.

Equally wise was the decision of the Byzantine em-

perors, first applied to Bulgaria, to allow the establishment of churches outside their borders. These were
largely autonomous, being only loosely tied to the
Patriarchate of Constantinople. This set the pattern for
the future. From now on, the Eastern Church was to
expand into Slavic lands beyond the Empire, in such
a way that its new converts were to be allowed to use
their own tongue, and to set up churches that were in
large measure independent. Hence, Slavic Europe was
to find accepting Eastern Christianity more advan-
tageous in many ways than accepting Christianity from
Rome, which demanded a large degree of subordination
and the use of Latin. Although Moravia, despite Cyril
and Methodius, eventually accepted Rome, most of the
rest of the Balkans and Russia came to look to Constantinople as the source of the Christianity that they
were to adopt. If the Church in the West found itself
in serious difficulties, in the East, Serbia and Bulgaria
were won for Christianity; a new era had begun for
the peoples of eastern Europe.

CULTURAL LIFE

The invasions that western Europe underwent naturally affected cultural life. Initially, the impetus that
stemmed from the Carolingian reforms was maintained.
This was particularly true in the heartland of the
Carolingian Empire, between the Loire and the Rhine.
Here a third generation of scholars emerged; they included John Scotus, a theologian of much originality,
who knew Greek; the historian Nithard; and the learned
ecclesiastical statesman, Archbishop Hincmar of Rheims.
In those monasteries in which the impetus of the Carolingian renaissance had remained strong, monastic annals continued to be kept. Gradually, however, even

this impetus faded. We see it first in Languedoc and Provence, where monastic annals stopped being written after the reign of Charles the Bald. Then, by the last decade of the century, the decline had spread to the regions of northern France and Belgium that were most affected by Viking attacks.

Some intellectual life, however, lingered on in cloisters that were located in the interior, away from the ravages of the invaders. Here clerical schools remained in operation, and annals continued to be composed. What did cease to exist in this part of Europe was central direction. The royal courts now abandoned the cultural role they had played at the time of Charlemagne and Louis the Pious; Charles the Bald was the last Carolingian monarch to act as a patron of learning. Arnulf in Germany was a powerful ruler, but in his eyes intellectual life had no special importance.

Even in Carolingian Italy, despite its prosperity, there is little evidence of intellectual vitality. Its harried monarchs could not serve as effective leaders in cultural development. A monk at Monte Cassino could write a relatively respectable history of the Lombards of Benevento, and the papal chancery maintained a fair standard of scholarship, especially during the time of Pope Nicholas I, but generally the level was low. Nor does the evidence indicate that things were much better in Christian Spain.

Indeed, the only Western country in which there was a revival of intellectual life was England. This was the result of an effort by Alfred the Great to remedy the cultural deficiencies of his people. It took place largely at his court, since by now Anglo-Saxon monasticism was moribund. Alfred personally took the initiative, by causing an Anglo-Saxon version of Orosius' *Seven Books of History Against the Pagans* to be composed, and by himself translating Gregory's *Pastoral Care*. He was responsible for beginning *The Anglo-Saxon Chronicle*, which was to become one of the great historical works of the Middle Ages. The use of Anglo-Saxon instead of Latin was a significant feature of this revival; there was little interest in those pagan classical Latin authors with whom Carolingian scholars had been so concerned. Nevertheless, here in England, by the early tenth century a center of intellectual life of some importance had again appeared.

More important than any intellectual development in western Europe, however, were those that took place in the Byzantine Empire. Here we suddenly find a remarkable outburst of intellectual activity, centered in a scholarly circle gathered about Bardas Caesar; it included in its number Photius and Leo the Grammarian. These men, closely connected with the Imperial court, showed an interest in Plato and other Greek classical authors who had been neglected for centuries. There was also a revival of interest in historiography: successors to Theophanes and Nicephorus wrote continuations to the works of the great historians of the sixth century. The Emperor Leo the Wise himself composed his *Tactica*, as a manual of military tactics that revised Maurice's *Strategycon*, as well as *The Book of the Prefect*, which described Byzantine economic controls in the Imperial capital.

The crowning achievement of this age in Byzantium, however, was a new law code called the *Basilics*, a complete revision of the Empire's law that replaced the earlier *Ecloga* and Justinian Code and dealt with the Church as well as the state. Nor was the revival confined to secular culture. During this period "Saints' Lives" were composed in large numbers, as were hymns and a complex type of church music. A church that was at last free of controversy began to appeal to the religious needs of the entire population.

ART AND ARCHITECTURE

In art and architecture there is less to show, since an age of invasion and disorder could not produce much in the way of creative activity. This is true even of military architecture. Most of the castles and fortifications that were built to oppose Viking and other invaders were simple towers, surrounded by ditches and palisades and constructed of wood. Only in Italy do we find exceptions to this rule. Here a more complex type of construction evolved, perhaps copied from Byzantium, in which use was made of motte and bailey—the forerunner of the more complex castle of later medieval times.

In art, the dislocations caused by the invasions gave rise to more specifically regional styles in certain areas of Europe. In northern France and Germany, manuscript illuminations indicate that the Carolingian style of the early ninth century, with its eclectic combination of traditions and its naturalistic emphasis, still retained its hold. But across the Channel a more distinctive Anglo-Saxon style appeared, as the result of the cultural advances that took place at Alfred's court. The most distinctive style of all, however, was to be seen in the churches that were built about the middle of the ninth century in Castile. Both the architecture and the decoration of these churches mark them as contributions to European art and architecture, matching in importance the churches built in Lombardy a century earlier. They also reveal an artistic sensibility that is distinctly Iberian.

The characteristic feature of northern Europe is the

diffusion of the Scandinavian style, which now spread from its homeland west to England and Ireland and east into Russia. Everywhere, it began to merge with the artistic traditions of the lands where the Scandinavians settled, bringing its interlaced dragon forms of jewelry and metalwork in its wake, and linking together the northern seas artistically, just as they were joined politically and economically.

Finally, in Byzantium, after the artistic darkness of the Iconoclast period, mosaics were again being used to decorate churches with their glowing colors, combining the traditions of Justinian's art with the somewhat different spirit of the age of the Macedonian emperors. A similar brilliance of color also appears in the illuminated manuscripts of the period, some of which display a renewed interest in classical forms that matches the classicism of the circle that surrounded Bardas Caesar. Byzantine art had at last come of age and developed canons of taste that were to influence many of its neighbors.

chapter V

A New Europe,

A.D. 911 – 1000

*B*y the year 1000, Europe as we know it in the Middle Ages had at last taken shape. Except along the shores of the Baltic and in parts of south Russia, tribal Europe had disappeared, to be replaced by a much more advanced system of political life. Equally important is the fact that Europe shared a common Christian civilization, except for Moslem Spain and a few areas of Scandinavia and the Baltic. It was its Christianity more than anything else that distinguished it from those other civilizations that lay to the south and east. And as Christianity and political cohesion became the order of the day, the older division of the continent into civilized and barbarian ceased to have any meaning. Instead, a complex political and cultural diversity took its place. Now Spaniards, French, Irish, English, Italians, Germans, Hungarians,

Poles, Swedes, Danes, Norwegians, Serbs, Bulgarians, and Russians were somehow beginning to differ from one another within an overall Christian civilization. The age of nations lay far in Europe's future, but already various areas were beginning to develop in such a way that they could form nations later on.

Political Divisions of Europe

THE BYZANTINE EMPIRE

Five states were particularly important among the political units into which Europe had been divided by the year 1000: the Byzantine Empire and Kievan Russia in the East; the Ottonian Empire in the center; and Ommayad Spain and England in the West. The Byzantine Empire was perhaps the most important, for under able emperors its power, which had begun to be revived in the late ninth century, continued throughout the tenth. Except for Basil II, these emperors were not members of the Imperial Macedonian family, but able military leaders associated with this house as co-emperors. The work of these men, Romanus Lecapenus, Nicephorus Phocas, and John Zimisces, was to expand the Empire's borders until, by the year 1000, it covered an area greater than any it had ruled over for some centuries.

This expansion was partly naval, as a new powerful fleet built by Romanus Lecapenus sailed into the Mediterranean in the 960s, to recover Cyprus and Crete and to patrol the western waters, around Sicily and southern Italy. In part, it was marked by the appearance of a new, aggressive, striking army which moved east to reconquer Cilicia and northern Syria and to fight a series of bloody wars against the Bulgarians in the Balkans. These western campaigns resulted in the conquest of part of Bulgaria by John Zimisces, and the rest soon after 1000 by Basil II. Now, for the first time since the Emperor Maurice, Byzantium's frontiers extended to the Danube. It had become a power in Italy, in Central Europe, in the Black Sea, and in much of the Mediterranean.

Military expansion, however, resulted in serious political, social, and economic problems. An aggressive army needed heavily armed cavalry to be effective, and this could best be recruited from a landed aristocracy that possessed large estates. Thus emperors of the period continued to favor such an aristocracy, which absorbed the tenures of its weaker neighbors and reduced them to dependence. Despite the efforts of Romanus Lecapenus to enforce them, laws forbidding this became dead letters, especially during the reigns of Nicephorus Phocas and John Zimisces. This led to a crisis during the early days of Basil II, who had to crush revolts that were led by the military aristocracy. By the year 1000, despite Basil's efforts, Byzantium had to face the serious internal problem of a military aristocracy whose interests were often opposed to those of the central government—a problem that was to prove all but fatal to the Empire in the next century.

Byzantium's new naval strength also created problems, since it mainly benefited such Italian trading cities as Venice, Amalfi, and Bari, which were nominally part of the Empire, but were determined to trade extensively with Moslem lands and with parts of Europe that were often hostile to Byzantium itself. By the year 1000, Venice was able to follow an all but independent policy, using her fleet to dominate the Illyrian shores of the Adriatic and trading widely beyond lands subject to the Empire. At the same time, these Italian cities had come to monopolize most of Byzantium's trade with western Europe. This problem of the Italian merchants and their relationship to the Empire was to vex Byzantine authorities in the centuries to come. Down to the year 1000, however, such problems had not yet become very acute, and Byzantium, wealthy and powerful on both land and sea, was able to exercise an influence on many parts of Europe, as it had not been able to do for centuries.

KIEVAN RUSSIA

Hardly less powerful was Kievan Russia, which had also emerged as a strong state during the last years of the ninth century. Its tenth-century rulers, Igor, Sviatoslav, and Vladimir, increased the strength of their principality, despite civil wars that sometimes made an orderly succession difficult. It was Sviatoslav who broke the power of the Kazars on the lower Volga, and alarmed Byzantium by attacking the Bulgars and attempting to extend his empire to the Danube. Although he was defeated by John Zimisces and killed by the Pecheneks in the steppes on his way back to Kiev, it was probably this campaign, like an earlier Russian attack on Constantinople in 944, that convinced the Byzantine rulers that they needed to come to terms with such dangerous neighbors. In Basil II's time, this resulted in a marriage alliance between Vladimir and Anna, the emperor's sister, under the terms of which the Kievan ruler accepted Christianity for himself and his people. By the year 1000, a Kievan Russia had come into existence that, despite nomad opposition, dominated a vast area, stretching from the Baltic to the Black and Caspian seas. Allied to Byzantium, and

Orthodox Christian in its religion, this Russian state had become a major political, economic, and cultural factor in tenth-century Europe.

THE OTTONIAN EMPIRE

Hardly less important than these two states was the new empire under German rule that emerged in Central Europe during this period. The revival of royal power in Germany may be dated from 919, when Henry, Duke of Saxony, was chosen king as successor to its Carolingian line. Upon accession, he found Germany troubled: most of the authority was in the hands of local dukes, and Magyars were raiding the land from their base in Hungary. Henry checked Hungarian raiders by building fortresses and raising a new army of heavily armed cavalry. He advanced north to seize Hedeby from the Danes, and sent powerful Saxon nobles east to expand German power into Slavic tribal areas beyond the Elbe. By the end of his reign, he had become so powerful that in 936 his son, Otto, succeeded him as king without much opposition.

Under Otto I, Henry's work of consolidation continued. In 955 he ended the threat of the Magyars by defeating them at the battle of Lechfeld; soon thereafter they ceased raiding, settled in Hungary, accepted Christianity, and became part of civilized Europe. Otto also extended his authority in the Baltic, and continued German expansion into Slavic lands in the east, the latter in alliance with the new Poland that was arising under Miezko. Nor did he neglect his western borders. He married as his first queen a sister of Aethelstan, the king of England; annexed Lorraine, which French rulers claimed as their own; and, by playing one side against the other in the French Capetian-Carolingian rivalry, limited France's ability to disturb his control over this duchy. Finally, he broke the power of the independent dukes of south Germany, and tied all the German duchies to him by a system of family alliances. Unlike his father, Otto relied on the Church, whose support was more dependable than that of the turbulent nobility. Like the Carolingians before him, he gave much land to bishops and abbots. In return, he required them to raise from their estates armies that would follow him into battle and to serve as administrators in his government.

The German Church furnished the principal military and administrative support for the realm, a fact that proved important when Otto, taking up the threads of Carolingian policy, began to intervene in Burgundy and Italy. His first expedition to Lombardy came in 951. When the Italian ruler Berenger intrigued against him, he was forced to intervene again, and finally, answering an appeal from the Pope, he marched south to Rome, where he was crowned Emperor in 962. The revival of a Western Empire, moribund since the time of Arnulf, had many consequences: it forced Otto and his immediate successors to concern themselves with the Papacy; it led to attempts to conquer Venice; and it embroiled German rulers with the Byzantine emperors, who were not willing to have their influence in Italy and papal Rome challenged by monarchs whom they regarded as upstarts, with little claim to an Imperial Roman title.

Moreover, embroilment in Italy had disastrous consequences north of the Alps. Under Otto II, Denmark was able to throw off the German yoke, and a great Slavic revolt almost eliminated German influence east of the Elbe. Otto III was able to reestablish some sort of hegemony over Slavic Central Europe only by recognizing the *de facto* independence of Poland, Bohemia, and Hungary, and their right to control their own churches.

Nor were the policies of the Ottos in Italy more successful. Otto II, by marrying a Byzantine bride of quasi-Imperial status, secured from Constantinople a grudging recognition of his Imperial title. But he failed to conquer Venice and southern Italy, which remained in Byzantium's sphere of influence. Otto III was filled with ideas of Imperial glory, and his partnership with Gerbert, whom he made Pope, resulted in some sonorous phrases about a Christian Empire, but little remained of Imperial power in Italy after his death in 1002. Again the Papacy fell into the hands of local Roman noble families, and Byzantium regained its influence over it. A tradition of German Imperial intervention in Italy had been created; that was all.

Nevertheless, the appearance of a strong tenth-century Empire on a Carolingian model was a political fact of importance. If it lost authority—especially in Italy— after the year 1000, it retained considerable influence elsewhere. It remained important for the Germans, who continued to support it, and for the Scandinavians and Slavs who were its neighbors. Without it, the history of the Church and of the Papacy would have been vastly different in the centuries to come.

OMMAYAD SPAIN

Of the other two important states in western Europe, England and Ommayad Spain, the emergence of the latter as a powerful realm is in some ways surprising. It seems to have been the result of two factors. One was the new prosperity that developed in Spain, as trade increased with the Moslem world of the Mediterranean, and new links were established with the gold of the Sudan. This gave the rulers of Cordova, for the first time, financial resources that they could use to create a strong army and navy. Secondly, in Abd-ar-Rahman III and Almansor, Moslem Spain found leaders who were able to make use of these armed forces in such a way that the Iberian Peninsula passed almost entirely under Cordova's influence and control.

This advance began during the reign of Abd-ar-Rahman, who assembled an army of slave and mercenary troops that gave him authority in Andalusia and Valencia. Then he moved north and broke the power of the independent lords of the Ebro valley. He finally extended his power into Morocco and in the Mediterranean, by building a powerful fleet that rivaled that of his Fatimid enemies in the Magreb. In the last years of his reign, he proclaimed himself caliph, the first Spanish Moslem ruler to bear that title. By this time, his power was so great that he was able to extend a protectorate over the Christian principalities in the north: Leon, Castille, Aragon, and Barcelona.

Under Almansor, who ruled as dictator some two decades later, Cordova continued to dominate the Iberian Peninsula, although more through naked force than diplomacy. Almansor was determined to make Christian rulers fear him, and he launched a number of great campaigns against them. One captured the great Christian shrine of Santiago de Compostela, while another resulted in the sack of Barcelona. Terrorized by this show of force, Christian Spain hastened to accept the overlordship of Cordova down to Almansor's death in 1002.

In the long run, however, this brutal use of force was to prove dangerous to Moslem Spain. It increased the power of the slave and mercenary troops upon whom Cordova depended for its strength, and it convinced northern Spanish rulers that they needed to increase their own military forces, in order to protect themselves in the future. Soon after Almansor's death, a series of revolts broke out in Cordova, as his armies tore asunder the state he had ruled so well, while on his northern frontiers Christian attacks were launched with a military strength that his policies had done so much to bring into being. All this, however, still lay in the future; down to the early eleventh century, Moslem Spain remained a remarkably powerful, prosperous, and well-governed state.

ANGLO-SAXON ENGLAND

Anglo-Saxon England developed slowly as a proto-national state, from the time of Alfred the Great to the last quarter of the tenth century, as English kings gradually conquered the Danelaw and asserted a general hegemony over much of the rest of Britain. During the course of reconquest, these rulers developed a unique political system, centered on the shires. These were administered, on the king's behalf, by sheriffs who were officials, not feudatories. There was also a national system of law, and a national nonfeudal army and navy. Further, the monarchy controlled the English Church and the minting of money on a national basis. Finally, when Danish raids were resumed, late in the tenth century, Aethelred the Redeless levied the first national taxes—the celebrated Danegelds. Possessing a well-organized chancery that was already issuing writs, England had the most centralized government in Europe beyond the borders of Moslem Spain and Byzantium.

Nevertheless, it needs to be emphasized that the political and social structure of England more nearly resembled that of Scandinavia than that of any other part of Europe. Her monarchs maintained close relations with the kings of Norway and Denmark, and looked toward the Baltic rather than south toward France. The age was already dawning that was to produce Canute in the next century.

OTHER STATES

These were not the only states in which political consolidation was under way. Scotland was slowly developing from its late ninth-century beginnings toward a somewhat greater unity by the first years of the eleventh century, while Wales in the tenth century found in Llewellyn the Great a chieftain who, for the first time in its history, was able to impose something akin to order on its tribal structure. Even Ireland, during these years, despite the presence of Viking principalities along its coasts, began to find in the institution of a "high king" the symbol of a unity it had seldom known earlier.

The same thing happened in Scandinavia. Norway remained united after the death of Harold Fairhair, who had created the Norwegian kingdom, while Sweden, by the time of Olaf Sköttkonung, showed a similar continuation of unity and the growth of royal authority. Denmark, however, was the Scandinavian country in which political development was most pronounced. Harold Bluetooth reunited and rather superficially Christianized the country so that, when his son Svein succeeded him, he was able to use it as a base from which he could dominate much of Norway and attack England.

In Central Europe also, the peoples began to form permanent political units that transcended tribal organization. A Polish state appeared under Miezko and Boleslas Chobry; a strong Bohemia emerged as successor to Greater Moravia; and, during the reign of St. Stephen, Hungary became an orderly part of Europe. The Serbs and the Croats found political unity under native princes. Central Europe, so long backward in a political sense, began to catch up with its neighbors.

Indeed, there was only one region that did not share in the trend toward political consolidation. That was France. Although in the next century France was to be the most influential political area in Europe, during these years it showed little political promise. The land that lay between the Pyrenees, the Alps, and the German kingdom continued to be as disorganized as it had been during the late ninth century. Nominally subject to a French monarch, but undermined by Carolingian-Capetian rivalry, and by a weak king of Provence-Burgundy, this part of Europe was actually ruled by its nobility, which, in increasingly feudal fashion, dominated local districts and ignored the rulers. In some areas, such as Flanders, Normandy, Anjou, and Provence, a few noble families were beginning by the year 1000 to create principalities that gave a political promise of order on a local basis. Elsewhere, a pattern of internal disorder was the rule.

France apart, the progress Europe made during this period is marked. From the Urals to the Atlantic, Europe had turned its back on its tribal past in order to achieve a new stage of political development. The dichotomy of civilized and uncivilized, Roman and barbarian, Christian and pagan had ended; a new Europe had emerged.

Economic Progress

TRADE

Progress in the economic realm more than matched the political advance. (See Map 4.) Its most important aspect was the extension of the great northern trading area that, by the year 900, already stretched from the British Isles to the Black and Caspian seas. Now this economic region grew in size, as Iceland and Ireland and Central Europe north of the Danube became part of it. Although the major trade routes that tied it together were still maritime and fluvial—the Irish, North, and Baltic seas, or rivers like the Scheldt, Rhine, Elbe, Vistula, Dvina, Dniepr, Volga, and Danube— terrestrial routes had also begun to come into their own. Particularly important were those that passed through Germany to Kiev, by way of Prague, Cracow, and Lvov; those that linked Hungary and the middle Danube region with the Baltic; and those that crossed the Alps from Germany and the Rhinelands to northern Italy.

The merchants who traveled along these routes belonged, in the main, to the same groups that had been important in Viking times—Anglo-Saxons, Frisians, Germans, Jews, and Scandinavians in the western portion; Jews, Scandinavians, Slavs, and Moslems in the eastern portion. By the year 1000, however, there was a growing tendency for some of these merchants to travel further from their homelands in the pursuit of gain. Anglo-Saxons, for instance, traded with lands in the eastern Baltic, and Germans began to appear in Russia in fairly large numbers, while both visited north Italian markets regularly, especially after 955, when the

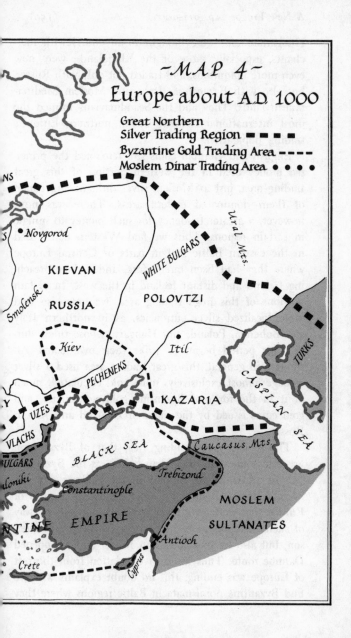

-MAP 4-
Europe about AD 1000

Great Northern
Silver Trading Region ▪ ▪ ▪ ▪
Byzantine Gold Trading Area ▬ ▬ ▬
Moslem Dinar Trading Area • • • •

Novgorod

KIEVAN

Smolensk

RUSSIA

WHITE BULGARS

POLOVTZI

Ural Mts.

Kiev

Itil

TURKS

PECHENEKS

UZES

KAZARIA

CASPIAN
SEA

VLACHS

BLACK SEA

Caucasus Mts.

BULGARS

Trebizond

loniki

Constantinople

MOSLEM

NTINE   EMPIRE

SULTANATES

Antioch

Crete

Cyprus

Hungarian raids were brought to an end. Jewish merchants, especially those of the Rhinelands, were now even more ubiquitous, and traded not only with Russia, but also with Byzantium, Italy, and Moslem Mediterranean lands. They and the Scandinavians formed the most international element within northern Europe's trading population.

English and German coins still remained the principal money used in the western portion of this great trading area, just as Moslem silver dirhems and copies of them dominated eastern areas. There was now, however, a greater tendency for such money to mingle in certain regions. Thus we find Western coins used in the eastern Baltic and in parts of Central Europe where they had been rare before, and dirhems reaching Ireland and distant Iceland in the west. In certain portions of this huge trading area, we now also find more localized silver currencies, as in northern Italy and Bohemia, Poland, and Hungary, whose rulers during this period began to strike their own coins. Although, in general, this great trading area used a silver coinage almost exclusively, some gold circulated, much of it in the form of Byzantine gold nomismata, and gold coins issued by the rulers of England and Kievan Russia.

The second great trading area, that of Byzantium, was also somewhat larger than before, as the Byzantine Empire expanded its borders in the Balkans and the Mediterranean. It now did more trade with regions of Europe that were on a silver standard, not only by way of such entrepôts as Naples-Amalfi, Venice, and Cherson, but also by way of Kievan Russia and a reopened Danube route. Thus its relative isolation from the rest of Europe was ending; this no doubt explains why we find Byzantine nomismata in Baltic regions where they had been unknown for centuries. Although it enjoyed active trade with the Moslem east, its European commerce was in the hands of non-Byzantine merchants—for the most part Italians, Jews, Russians, and Slavs—which gave it a generally passive economic character.

The third great trading area was the Moslem. Spain, Sicily, and North Africa in the western Mediterranean had now become part of a great dinar area that included Syria, Egypt, and the Moslem Middle East. The prosperity of Moslem Spain, based on industry, trade, and agriculture, had spread northward by the year 1000, until both the Asturian Christian kingdoms and Catalonia were part of this economic region. Moslem merchants from Spain, Sicily, and North Africa were the principal active traders in the area, although some Jews—in particular, from Spain—participated in its commerce. It was chiefly by way of Amalfi and Naples on Italy's west coast and Venice in the Adriatic that this Moslem Mediterranean area still traded with the great northern trading region that had emerged by the end of the tenth century.

France and the coast of northwestern Italy remained economically isolated from the three great trading regions just described throughout most of the tenth century, as they had in the ninth. Here economic life was still local in character, matching the area's political fragmentation—except perhaps for Normandy, where international trade was more active. As the year 1000 approached, however, the situation began to change. Traffic with Ireland, Britain, and the Low Countries, all part of the great northern trading region, increased. Merchants from northern France began to join German and English ones in the markets of northern Italy, while Jewish traders from Verdun, Vienne, Arles, and Narbonne traveled to Moslem Spain in larger numbers.

Moslem pirates were expelled from Provence in 972, and new life began to pervade older centers, such as Marseilles and Narbonne, and new towns like Montpellier along the Mediterranean shores. Commerce increased along the Rhone, Garonne, Loire and Seine, and Genoese and Pisans took to the sea again, first as pirates and then as merchants, tapping the trade of the western Mediterranean that the Moslems had so long controlled. Slowly at first and then swiftly, this last remaining isolated part of Europe began to join in the economic growth that was to characterize the next few centuries.

The situation that had developed in the Mediterranean by the tenth century explains why the Italians now became as important as merchants as were the Scandinavians, Jews, Germans, and Anglo-Saxons in the northern part of the continent. Connected, by way of Alpine passes, with the great northern trading region, the Italians could also trade freely with both Byzantium and the Moslem worlds. Thus, by the year 1000, they had replaced the Byzantines as the great middlemen who linked northern and western Europe with the eastern regions of the Mediterranean. And as France again became integrated into the rest of Europe, the Pisans and the Genoese began to join the Venetians in this middleman's role, upon which the future prosperity of Italy was to be based.

As commerce increased, along trade routes that linked trading areas or led to the Moslem east, a large variety of wares began to be carried by merchants to local and international markets. Many of these products were now industrial in nature, like the silks and brocades of Byzantium, Sicily, and Andalusia, the woolens of Flanders and England, the linen of Ireland and Russia, or the arms produced in Spain, the Rhinelands,

Austria, and northern Italy. Or else they were the mercury, tin, copper, lead, iron, and silver that Europe's mines produced in growing volume; or they represented natural products, such as wine, wheat, furs, timber, honey, wax, fish, and slaves, which were in great demand in both regional and international markets. By comparison with that of Merovingian and Carolingian times, the pattern had become increasingly complex.

In the same way, the simple trading stations of earlier periods grew in size and importance. By the year 1000, we can begin to think of them as towns in every area of Europe. Their characteristic feature was a reasonably large number of merchants and artisans who had settled as permanent residents and for the first time appear as a distinct class in society, differing from the peasantry and the landed proprietors of the surrounding countryside. By the year 1000, most of Europe had begun to develop a middle class, whose importance was to increase in coming centuries.

AGRICULTURE AND TECHNOLOGY

At the same time, there is evidence of continuing agricultural progress in the countryside, as the Carolingian revolution, which had been interrupted for a time in many regions, again began to gather force. An important new stimulus to such agrarian growth was the demand for foodstuffs from the growing towns. It resulted in Europe's peasants renewing their efforts to cut down the primeval forest, drain the marshes, and cultivate unoccupied wasteland. As they did so, peasant colonists moved south toward the Ebro valley in Spain, cultivated abandoned land in Dauphiné and Provence, edged their way toward the Welsh mountains in the English Midlands, and renewed their efforts to make the bottom lands of the Weser and Danube valleys productive. They became active in reclaiming forest land in Bohemia, in the Jutland peninsula, and in central Russia. Much still remained to be done, but by the year 1000 the peasantry were again transforming the European countryside into a more fertile and productive area.

Nor did technology lag behind. In northern Europe the heavy, wheeled plough and the horse collar spread over a wider area, while better ships were built for both warlike and trading purposes. Both Anglo-Saxon England and Scandinavia now began to construct large, turreted warships known as "dragon ships," and the design of Frisian cogs and Norse trading ships improved, enabling the latter to venture as far west as Greenland and the American continent. In the Mediterranean, where the lateen rig and the double pulley were improving sailing efficiency, Byzantium built better warships; this helps to explain why she again became a naval power in the tenth century. But it was the Italians who seem to have benefited most from these and other improvements in technology that had been pioneered in the Byzantine and Moslem worlds.

The Social Sphere

LANDOWNERS

It is somewhat surprising that there were relatively few changes in the social sphere to match the changes in the political and economic patterns. The new middle class that had appeared in the towns of the period was still so small, except in Italy, that it was not yet able to exert any great influence. And while there were a few regions where the peasants, who were breaking new ground to the plough, enjoyed greater freedom, these were the exceptions to the general rule, which made most peasants subject instead to control by the landed aristocracy.

Europe, in fact, continued to be dominated by a nobility of large landowners, as had been the case earlier. This aristocracy, now thoroughly militarized and increasingly feudal, had at its disposal more resources than had been the case earlier, for it could tap an increasing wealth in trade and commerce, and profit from the work of assarting, or clearing land, and colonization. Its members could thus afford the expensive castles and military equipment that permitted them to dominate many parts of Europe. Their number grew, especially in France, but also in Italy, Spain, and the Byzantine Empire. Henry the Fowler's new emphasis upon a heavily armed cavalry increased their number in Germany. Thus, by the early eleventh century, we find a Europe in which the nobility's influence was for a period to dominate the political and social scene, and to make the next two centuries an age of feudalism and upper-class militarism. By the year 1000, Europe was producing in large numbers the kind of aristocracy that was to follow William the Conqueror into England, tear asunder the Byzantine Empire, and seize from Islam areas in Moslem Spain, Sicily, and Syria.

THE CHURCH

As this new society emerged, the Church also recovered from the setbacks of the previous century and became more active. One aspect of this was its work in continuing the conversion of the pagan peoples of Europe. As noted earlier, the Eastern Church converted the Bulgars and Serbs in the late ninth century. Now an even greater victory was won, in the conversion of Russia. This began when Olga, of the Kievan royal house, accepted Christianity about the middle of the tenth century. Her son Sviatoslav, however, refused to follow her example, and it was not until the reign of Vladimir that orthodox Christianity finally won over the ruler of the Kievan state, who welcomed Byzantine monks to his realm and began the conversion of his people. Europe's largest remaining pagan state had at last become Christian.

Meanwhile, the Latin Church was equally successful in western Slavic regions, where Cyril and Methodius had already done much of the spadework. St. Adalbert of Prague, a member of a noble Czech family, was largely responsible for the success of this venture. After some years of effort, he persuaded Bohemia and Moravia to accept Christianity and communion with Rome. Then, driven from his homeland by political opponents, he fled to Poland. Here he was welcomed by the Polish royal house, which soon accepted Latin Christianity for itself and its people. He went on to meet a martyr's death a few years later, in an attempt to spread the Gospel among the heathen Prussians to the northeast of Poland.

A few years later, the Western Church gained still another part of Central Europe for Christianity. By the first years of the tenth century, western missionaries had begun the conversion of the Croats, although the Hungarians still remained pagan. Soon after the battle of Lechfeld, however, this began to change. Western missionaries were welcomed in Hungary and the Magyars—like the Croats, Bohemians, Slovaks, and Poles—became Christian. Thus, by the year 1000, the Christianization of Slavic eastern Europe had been completed, the western portion accepting communion with Rome, the eastern area receiving its Christianity from Constantinople.

The conversion of Scandinavia took place almost simultaneously. In the late tenth century, if we can believe the Jelling Stone, which records the matter in runic characters, Harold Bluetooth completed the Christianization of Denmark and organized his land into bishoprics. The Viking kings of Ireland became Christian at about the same time. Norway and Sweden, however, lagged behind Denmark. The turning point came when Olaf Tryggvason, king of Norway, became a Christian. Soon after, in the time of St. Olaf, the Norwegian people abandoned paganism for the Christian faith. Their contemporaries in Sweden quickly followed suit and, though a few pagan enclaves remained here and in Iceland and western Norway, by the year 1000 the conversion of Scandinavia was substantially complete. Indeed, in all of Europe only the Baltic and Finnish tribal peoples still clung to a paganism that had disappeared elsewhere.

Recovery after the Viking and Magyar invasions, as well as the expansion of Christianity, naturally benefited the monasteries, although they were still handicapped by the control exercised by the secular aristocracy. In England, St. Dunstan continued Alfred's work of reforming old monasteries and founding new ones, and in Germany the Ottonian House supported such abbeys as Hersfeld. But paradoxically, it was in disunited and politically feudalized France and Lorraine that Western monasticism began to evolve in new ways. Here, after a period of decadence, abbeys were again established in such regions as Gascony, Dauphiné, and Provence, from which they had all but disappeared. And at Cluny a new and different type of monastic system emerged, which was to set the pattern for Western monasticism during the following period. The Cluniac system demanded that monasteries should be freed of secular control and grouped into a congregation that was ruled by the abbot of a central monastery. It was the Church's reply to feudal anarchy, assuring the individual houses freedom from feudal control, and giving them a stronger mode of organization, which would make their work really effective.

The secular Church, on the other hand, was dominated by the great noble families, who regarded Church offices as their property and tended to fill them with candidates who were unqualified to hold them. This was less true in Germany and England than elsewhere, for here the rulers came to control the Church and to fill its offices with men of somewhat higher caliber. In the Western Church as a whole, however, the hierarchy was increasingly secularized and feudalized, and incapable of giving proper leadership.

To this, the Papacy was no exception. By the early tenth century, as noted earlier, it had come to be controlled by noble families in Rome. It was corrupt, and subject to Byzantine influence, and had lost its ability to give direction to the Western Church as a whole. To a certain extent, Otto I's conquest of northern and central Italy and his assumption of the title of emperor changed this state of affairs. He and his Imperial successors periodically used their influence to see that better Popes were chosen, often men who were non-Italians, of whom Gerbert of Rheims, later Pope Sylvester II, was perhaps the leading example. But Imperial influence in Rome was at best intermittent, and reforming Popes gave way quite frequently to others who were the nominees of the corrupt Roman nobility. Hence it was hardly before the time of Leo IX (1047–1056) that the Papacy, with the help of the Emperor Henry III, could take the lead in providing the Western Church with an enlightened and spiritual Christian leadership.

The Orthodox Church showed greater resilience. Although the emperors still insisted on controlling the Church, there is no doubt that the patriarchs of Constantinople now began to enjoy a new importance. The refusal of a patriarch to sanction the fourth marriage of Leo VI was one sign of this; another was the prohibition of a marriage between the Empress Theophano and John Zimisces. If he was backed by the force of public opinion, the patriarch could now successfully defy an emperor. The role of the powerful Michael Cerularius was already foreshadowed.

During these years, Eastern monasticism, like that in the West, began to take on a special organized form that was to affect its future. It first appeared at Mt. Athos, where bodies of monks, each body enjoying autonomy, grouped themselves together in one large area that was carefully isolated from the secular world beyond. The popularity of this new kind of monastic system, as well as of abbeys of the older sort, continued in the Byzantine Empire. They were endowed with large tracts of land, given them by the faithful, to such an extent that Basil II thought it necessary to legislate against such accumulations of property in monastic hands. Nevertheless, the zeal and vigor of the monks of the Eastern Church continued to be a feature of this period; their influence spread beyond the boundaries of the Empire into newly converted Slav lands, where monasteries took firm root and helped instill Christianity among the population.

The Progress of Learning

IN WESTERN EUROPE

Among the areas where cultural progress was taking place, Moslem Spain was outstanding. While this had not hitherto been the case, the situation had changed when some of the best scholars of the Moslem East were attracted to Spain by the generous support offered them by the wealthy rulers of Cordova. These same rulers also began to accumulate scholarly libraries, which encouraged intellectual pursuits. Thus Moslem Spain laid the foundation for its later eminence as a center of Arabic philosophy and science. Particularly interesting is the role that Spanish Jews began to play in interpreting and adding to this culture. We also find here a new and distinctive literary tradition developing, best exemplified by a poem called "The Ring-Necked Dove." This tradition stressed poetry, written in the Spanish vernacular, that mingled romance with a high-minded platonism to celebrate love between a man and his lady, thus anticipating the troubadour tradition of southern France of the following century.

As Moslem Spain developed as a major center of culture, it began to influence Christian Spain to the north, which, during this period, was under Cordova's influence. It was at the abbey of Ripoll in Catalonia that Gerbert became acquainted with the superior scientific and intellectual learning of Moslem Spain, which he carried back with him to the cathedral schools of northern France. This is the first proof we possess that western Europe was beginning to be affected by the Moslem culture of the time; it was to be followed by much borrowing in the centuries to come.

Anglo-Saxon England during this same period continued to develop its culture along lines already laid down in the time of Alfred the Great. Various versions of the *Anglo-Saxon Chronicle* were written in the monasteries of England; monastic schools were active; and a rich secular and religious literature was composed in the Anglo-Saxon tongue, much of it being poetry. Alfred's successors continued to develop Anglo-Saxon law, as each added to the existing corpus his own special enactments, while the chanceries of Aethelstan and his successors turned out charters that show an administrative competence of a high order.

In Ottonian Germany, intellectual traditions from Carolingian times remained alive. Indeed, by the late tenth century, intellectual activity at the Ottonian court had become so intense that some have referred to this period as the Ottonian Renaissance. The Saxon emperors gave to culture a direction it had long lacked in their domains, by encouraging scholars and cathedral and monastic schools. Although the content of this culture was little changed from that which had prevailed in Charlemagne's time, we find monastic and Church annals being kept; among the more important of these were the annals of Widukind and Thietmar of Merseburg, who celebrated the accomplishments of the Saxon line, and others that give us a particular view of developments in Scandinavia and the Baltic. More remarkable is the figure of Roswitha, who, in a remote nunnery, produced plays derived from those of Terence.

In northern France also, a tradition of education survived, despite the disorders of the period. The cathedral schools of Verdun and Rheims, where Gerbert taught, continued to train scholars; Richer carried forward the tradition of writing chronicles that had been begun at the time of the Carolingians, and Dudo of St. Quentin related events on the local Norman scene. If monastic learning seems disappointing south of the Loire, biographies such as St. Odo's *Life of St. Gerald of Aurillac* still offer a vivid picture of the life of the period. In much of this part of Europe, the work of Charlemagne and Alfred continued to inspire their tenth-century successors, thus forming a link between the Carolingian age and that which was to emerge in the late eleventh century.

While learning continued to be essentially clerical north of the Alps, in Italy during this same period, it was more secular in character. In Lombardy, town schools had begun to emerge, to train a growing middle class in the elements of grammar and logic necessary for business success, and in Venice the first of those town histories or chronicles was being composed that were to be such a feature of Italian intellectual life in succeeding centuries. Liudprand of Cremona, in his history of the period, especially in Italy, and in his story of his embassy to Constantinople, shows the importance of a class of educated laymen in the Italy of the tenth century, who differed in so many ways from those learned churchmen that still dominated northern European intellectual life.

IN BYZANTIUM

It is, of course, Byzantium that shows the clearest evidence of a vigorous intellectual life during this period. Here interest in Plato and classical Greek authors, unknown in the West, continued throughout the tenth century, and became the basis of a revival of Platonism in the writings of Psellus and at the University of Constantinople, some decades later. Historians continued to chronicle their times, and a second scholarly emperor, Constantine Porphyrogenitus, composed his *Book of Ceremonies* and *De Thematibus*, which provide a vivid view of the workings of Byzantine administration and diplomacy. Science, medicine, and literary interests attracted a large number of gifted scholars to the capital, while the poem *Digenes Akritas*, written in a more colloquial Greek, is an example of the popular romances that were enjoyed by an even wider audience. No wonder Kievan Russia found in Byzantium so much inspiration toward developing its own cultural and legal traditions.

Architecture and Creativity

Throughout Europe, the tenth century was a great age of building. In Moslem Spain, at Cordova and Seville, a new Moorish architecture developed, which set the style for much of this region's later building; in the north, Christian Spain continued to build churches and abbeys in a distinctive style that had been begun in the mid-ninth century. At the same time, frescos in Catalonia mirror a world that was beginning to express itself in its own local idiom.

Hardly less important was the development of other regional styles of architecture in the West. In Lombardy and Tuscany, a number of churches built during this period reveal a style that represents a revival of many of the elements of classical architecture and sculpture. At Venice, on the other hand, Byzantine influence pervades the scene, as is seen in the altar screen that is still preserved in St. Mark's Cathedral. In Germany, another group of distinctive churches were built in places like Reichenau, laying the basis for the later German Romanesque architecture; in Kiev, churches began to be built in a style, much influenced by Byzantium, that was still typically Russian.

In England and central France, the period witnessed the rise of distinct forms of architecture that owed even less to classical and Byzantine inspiration than to that of Ottonian Germany. Some small parish churches reveal that a distinctive English architecture had begun to emerge, while in France the great abbey of Cluny, begun at mid-century, marks the inauguration of a special French Romanesque style that was later to develop so gloriously.

This was an age of great artistic creativity. The Byzantine mosaics of Hagia Sophia show a continued use of brilliant colors in a style that had been inaugurated at the time of Leo the Wise, and was now spreading to more provincial centers outside the capital. The manuscripts of the period, such as the *Joshua Roll*, are another example of that oriental love of color and those classical motifs that reflect the special nature of tenth-century Byzantine civilization. Manuscript illuminations in England and Ottonian Germany show that each country had now developed its own special artistic style, linked to the earlier Carolingian age, yet distinctly different. Even in Moslem Spain, we see in Mozarabic manuscripts a local Christian artistic tradition, which remained vigorous beneath the surface of a Moorish civilization. These local traditions of art matched the varied intellectual ones and were to produce the rich civilization of the high Middle Ages.

Conclusion

*T*he eleventh century dawned on a new European civilization that, after more than half a millennium, had emerged out of what had once been Roman and barbarian Europe. This new Europe was a blend of diverse traditions, peoples, and cultures. Even the Christianity that most of its peoples had come to share was about to be divided into competing Eastern and Western Churches. Its political forms were now diverse, ranging from the complex, advanced governments already found in Byzantium, Moslem Spain, and England to the simpler neo-Carolingian system of Germany, and the new monarchies in Poland, Denmark, and Kievan Russia, where power rested largely in warbands located at the courts of its rulers. Its economic life, based on three great trading regions—Moslem, Byzantine, and northern European—was equally diverse; it was only beginning to be integrated, to form a larger economic unity. Its urbanism, which was now increasing fairly rapidly, was already marked by differences between the towns of Flanders and Italy, which possessed a certain measure of independence, and those in Byzantium, Moslem Spain, and England, which were largely controlled by the central government. The special feature of Europe in its economic and political life was its variety and diversity, and the same thing was true of its cultural development.

Even while we emphasize Europe's positive achievements during this period, however, it would be wise to temper our enthusiasm for its progress. In the late tenth and the early eleventh century, life still remained brutal and difficult for all. The names given many of its rulers reveal the shocking nature of the political power they exercised—witness Eric Blood-Axe of York and Norway, William Iron-Arm of Toulouse, Fulk the Shark of Anjou, or Basil the Bulgarian Slayer of Byzantium. How plaintive are the words of a Christian chronicler of northern Spain, who, after seeing his region plundered by the Moslem armies of Cordova can write, "In this year [1002] died Almansor [Cordova's ruler] and was buried in Hell!" In the early eleventh century, the Papacy remained in the hands of a degraded Roman nobility, and an Adalbert could still find martyrdom at the hands of European pagans. Famines abound in the records left us by chroniclers, and learning was still the exception. Europe had advanced, but it still had a long way to go. We need to keep this clearly in mind.

Yet, granting all this, there *was* progress in this new Europe which had emerged and which, as these pages have tried to make clear, was no sudden affair, but a slow process, covering a number of centuries, in which each age—Barbarian, Merovingian, Carolingian, Viking, and Ottonian—played a significant role. It was also affected by periods of decline and stagnation that attended some area or other in almost every period we have considered. If Britain lagged in the fifth century, Italy did so in the late sixth, Byzantium in the late seventh and eighth, Spain in the ninth, and France in the tenth. Viewed as a whole, however, no age is entirely lacking in evidences of political, economic, and cultural growth. By the year 1000, Europe had emerged as a real center of civilization. The story of Europe during this period is not one of a dark age followed by a sudden recovery, but of a developing civilization.

Suggestions for
Further Reading

Three books are particularly worth study, although they concentrate too exclusively upon western Europe. These are: Henri Pirenne, *Mohammed and Charlemagne* (London: Allen & Unwin, 1939); Alfons Dopsch, *The Economic and Social Foundations of Western Civilization* (London: Routledge, 1953); and Christopher H. Dawson, *The Making of Europe* (New York: Macmillan, 1932). They should be supplemented by J. M. Wallace-Hadrill, *The Barbarian West* (New York: Harpers, 1952)* and *The Long-Haired Kings* (New York: Barnes & Noble, 1962) for western Europe, and by George Ostrogorsky, *History of the Byzantine State* (New Brunswick: Rutgers University Press, 1957) and Francis Dvornik, *The Making of Central and Eastern Europe* (London: Polish Research Center, 1949) for eastern Europe.

Other important works are Heinrich Fichtenau, *The Carolingian Empire* (Oxford: Blackwell, 1957) and Lucien Musset, *Les Peuples scandinaves au moyen age* (Paris: Presses Universitaires de France, 1951). Valuable recent regional studies are Dorothy White-

* Available in paperback editions.

lock, *The Beginnings of English Society* (Harmondsworth: Penguin, 1952;* Claudio Sánchez-Albornoz, *España, un enigma histórico*, Vol. I (Buenos Aires: Editorial Sudamericana, 1956); Archibald R. Lewis, *The Development of Southern French and Catalan Society, 718–1050* (Austin: The University of Texas Press, 1965); Geoffrey Barraclough, *The Origins of Modern Germany* (Oxford: Blackwell, 1962); Steven Runciman, *A History of the First Bulgarian Empire* (London: G. Bell and Sons, 1930); George Vernadsky, *Kievan Russia* (New Haven: Yale University Press, 1955); and D. M. Dunlop, *The History of the Jewish Kazars* (Princeton: Princeton University Press, 1954).

For economic developments, Archibald R. Lewis, *Naval Power and Trade in the Mediterranean*, A.D. 500–1100 (Princeton: Princeton University Press, 1951) and *The Northern Seas*, A.D. 300–1100 (Princeton: Princeton University Press, 1958) should be supplemented by different views to be found in Robert Latouche, *Birth of Western Economy* (London: Methuen, 1961) and Robert S. Lopez, *Naissance de l'Europe* (Paris: Colin, 1962), which is soon to appear in an English edition. Feudalism in its early aspects is best treated in François L. Ganshof, *Feudalism* (New York: Harpers, 1961)* and Joseph R. Strayer, *Feudalism* (Princeton: Van Nostrand, 1965),* while technological developments are surveyed in Lynn T. White, *Medieval Technology and Social Change* (Oxford: Clarendon Press, 1962).*

An adequate broad survey of the Church is found in Henry Daniel-Rops, *The Church and the Dark Ages, 406–1050* (New York: Dutton, 1959). See also Walter Ullmann, *The Growth of Papal Government in the Middle Ages* (London: Methuen, 1962) for the Papacy, and Richard W. Southern, *The Making of the Middle Ages* (New Haven: Yale University Press, 1953)* for the Church's intellectual role. A fine work on the Jews is Bernard Blumenkranz, *Juifs et Chrétiens dans le* *monde occidental, 430–1096* (Paris: Mouton and Co., 1960).

The earlier period of western Europe's cultural and intellectual development is brilliantly covered in Pierre Riché, *Education et culture dans l'occident barbare, VIe–VIIIe siècles* (Paris: Editions du Seuil, 1962), although Eleanor S. Duckett, *Gateway to the Middle Ages*, 3 vols. (Ann Arbor: University of Michigan Press, 1961)* is also worth serious study, as is David Knowles, *The Evolution of Medieval Thought* (New York: Random House, 1964).* Steven Runciman's *Byzantine Civilization* (London: Arnold, 1933)* provides the best treatment of culture in eastern Europe. For art and architecture see David Talbot-Rice, *The Art of Byzantium* (New York: Abrams, 1959); Rufus C. Morey, *Early Christian Art* (Princeton: Princeton University Press, 1953); Roger Hinks, *Carolingian Art* (Ann Arbor: University of Michigan Press, 1964);* and Nicholas Pevsner, *An Outline of European Architecture* (Harmondsworth: Penguin, 1953).*

◆§ *Index* §◆

Abassid caliphs, 78
Abd-ar-Rahman I, 78, 90, 116
Abd-ar-Rahman III, Caliph, 143
Adalbert of Prague, St., 156, 166
Adamman, 72
Adoptionist heresy, 101
Aethelstan, King, 140, 161
Agriculture, development of, 55–56, 57, 96–97, 124–25, 151, 153–54
Aix-la-Chapelle, 76, 80, 84, 101, 105, 108
Alcuin, 100, 104, 105, 106
Alemanni, 5, 8, 10, 11, 28, 81
Alfred the Great, 112, 118, 125, 127, 128–33, 132–33, 134, 144, 161, 162
Almansor, 143, 144, 166
Amalfi, 138, 150
Anastasius, Emperor, 26
Andalusia, 41, 43, 90, 143
Anglo-Saxon Chronicle, The, 133, 161
Anglo-Saxon law codes, 72
Anglo-Saxons, 7, 8, 10, 12, 13, 39, 46, 47, 50, 58, 59, 96, 104, 132, 134, 144–45, 147, 152, 161
Anjou, 146

Anskar, St., 80, 100, 128
Antas, 11
Aquitaine, 81
Arabs, 41, 42, 44, 45, 48, 60, 67, 78, 84, 87, 89, 90, 119
Aragón, 79, 143
Architecture, 35–36, 73, 107, 108–9, 134–35, 163–64
Arianism, 4, 22, 27, 30, 43, 44, 63, 66, 101
Aristotle, 32
Arnulf of Metz, St., 70, 117, 126, 132
Art, 36–37, 73–74, 107–9, 134–35, 164
Asia Minor, 9, 84, 85, 89
Askold, 113
Asturias, 116, 151
Athelred the Redeless, 144
Augustine, St., 33–34
Augustus, Emperor, 3
Austrasia, 43, 81
Avars, 9, 10, 12, 39, 41, 44–45, 47, 56, 60, 62, 80, 91, 93

Balearics, 115
Balkans, 8, 12, 13, 16, 40, 41, 76, 79, 80, 84, 90, 131, 138

Baltic area, 91, 93, 96, 110, 123, 136, 140, 145, 150

Barbarian Europe, 4–5, 77; changes in, 6–7; Church in (400–565), 25–31; cultural life (400–565), 31–37; economic developments (400–565), 11–21, (565–718), 47–57; intellectual activity in, 34–35; movements of peoples, 8–9; political power, problems of (400–565), 7–11; social relations (400–565), 22–25

Barcelona, 143

Bardas Caesar, 133, 135

Bari, 115, 138

Basil, St., 29

Basil I, Emperor, 119, 126, 129

Basil II, Emperor, 137, 138, 139, 159, 166

Basilics, 133

Basques, 12, 13, 99

Bavaria, 10, 16, 59, 61, 81

Bavarian law codes, 70

Bede, Venerable, 72, 100, 104

Belgium, 15, 20, 51

Belisarius, 23, 25

Benedict, St., 28, 30, 100

Benevento, 44, 79, 81

Beowulf, 35

Berbers, 78, 90

Black Sea, 138

Bluetooth, Harold, 145, 157

Boethius, 32, 33, 68

Bohemia, 8, 61–62, 118, 142, 146, 150, 154, 156

Boniface, Pope, 62, 82

Book of Durrow, 74

Book of Kells, 109

Book of the Prefect, 124, 133

Breviary of Alaric, 33

British Isles, 10, 13, 15, 17–20, 29, 30, 34, 35, 39, 46, 47, 48, 49, 50, 51, 58, 59, 61, 62, 64, 71–72, 76, 92, 96, 104, 112, 118, 119, 122, 123, 125, 126, 127, 132–33, 135, 144–45, 147, 151, 154, 157, 161, 164, 166. *See also* Anglo-Saxons; Ireland; Scotland; Wales

Brittany, 12, 13, 81

Bubonic plague, 12, 13

Bulgarian Empire, 118–19, 120, 131, 138

Bulgars, 9, 40, 45, 47, 60, 62, 79, 80, 84, 87, 88, 97, 113, 118–19, 139, 156

Burgundian law, 23, 33, 70

Burgundy and the Burgundians, 7, 10, 11, 13, 16, 141

Byzantine Empire (718–840), 54, 84–87; architecture in, 107; art in, 107–8; attacks on, 113; cultural life in, 107–8; economic changes in, 88–89; military developments in, 86–87; political repercussions to invasions in, 119–20; (911–1000), 137–40, 142, 150–51, 154, 162–63

Byzantium, 25, 42, 44, 45, 46, 49, 54, 56, 60, 67, 73, 75, 76, 80, 81, 86, 87, 88, 91, 96, 97, 99, 111, 113, 114, 115, 119, 120, 122, 126, 133, 135, 166

Caesarius of Arles, 34

Caesaropapism, 26–27, 101, 102, 128, 129

Carolingian Empire (718–840), 58, 62, 70, 73, 76–84, 85, 86, 88, 91, 128, 153; agriculture in, 96–97;

architecture in, 108; art in, 108–9; Church and, 82, 99–102; cultural life in, 103–6; disintegration of, 110, 116–18; economic changes in, 92–99; emergence of, 77–84; expansion and decline of, 81–82; government of, institutions of, 83–84; invasion of, 111–12, 117; landowners and, 83; political repercussions to invasions of, 116–18

Carolingian Renaissance, 105–6, 131

Cassiodorus, 17, 28, 32–33, 68, 72

Castile, 134, 143

Castle construction, 125–26, 155

Catalonia, 90, 100, 116, 125, 127, 151, 160, 163

Celts, 10, 12, 13, 37

Central Europe, 20, 40, 47, 56, 88, 90–91, 93, 117, 122–23, 138, 140, 145–46, 147, 150, 156

Charlemagne, Emperor, 76, 80, 82, 83, 86, 91, 92, 93, 96, 98, 99, 101, 102, 104, 105, 108, 162

Charles the Bald, King, 116, 117, 132

Charles the Simple, King, 112, 117

Cherson, 88, 91, 150

China, 56, 57, 77, 92

Christian Church, *see* Greek Church; Latin Church

Chronicle of Fredegar, 69

Chronicle of the Popes, 68

Class distinctions, 58–60, 98, 99

Clovis, King, 9–10, 11, 28, 43

Cluny, 157–58, 164

Constans II, Emperor, 42, 44, 60, 63–64

Constantine IV, Emperor, 48, 54, 64

Constantine V, Emperor, 80, 84, 85, 102, 103

Constantine Porphyrogenitus, Emperor, 163

Constantinople, 7, 9, 12, 22, 23, 25, 31, 39, 42, 45, 48, 54, 56, 60, 63, 66, 67, 76, 84, 88, 89, 102, 108, 113, 115, 124, 142

Cordova, 78, 79, 90, 116, 143, 144, 160, 163

Corsica, 115

Council of Aix-la-Chapelle (816), 101

Council of Chalcedon (451), 26, 64

Council of Ephesus (431), 26

Council of Whitby (664), 61

Crete, 87, 115, 122, 137

Croats, 146, 156

Cultural progress, 67–75, 103–6, 107–8, 131–34, 160–63

Cyprus, 137

Cyril, St., 62, 130, 131, 156

Czechoslovakia, 13

Dagobert, King, 42, 43, 45, 70

Danegelds, 144

Danelaw, 112, 118, 129, 144

Dauphiné, 153, 157

Decretals, 128

Denmark and the Danes, 46, 50, 80, 81, 92, 93, 100, 111, 118, 126, 129, 140, 141, 144, 145, 157

Dependence, 24–25

Digenes Akritas, 163

Dir, 113

Dublin, 112, 118

Dunstan, St., 157

Dyle, Battle of the (892), 126

Eastern Church, *see* Greek Church

Eastern Roman Empire, 67–68, 78, 79. *See also* Byzantine Empire

East Frankish kingdom, 116, 117, 118

Ecloga, 133

Economic developments, 11–21, 47–57, 87–99, 147–54

Education, 105, 132, 160–63

Edward the Elder, King, 112, 118, 125

Egbert of Wessex, 79–80, 93

Egypt, 9, 26, 41, 77, 121, 151

Einhard, 101, 106

England, *see* British Isles

English Church, 144

Europe, new (911–1000): architecture and creativity, 163–64; economic progress, 147–54; learning, progress of, 160–63; political divisions of, 137–46; social sphere, 154–59

Fairhair, Harold, 114, 145

Famines, 166

Farmers' Law, 68–69

Feudalism, 99, 117, 125–26, 128, 155

Flanders, 13, 127, 146

Fortunatus, 70

France and the French, 15, 20, 30, 49, 62, 64, 92, 96, 99, 100, 104, 112, 122, 123, 125, 127, 146, 151, 152, 155, 157, 161–62, 164, 166

Franks, 5, 7, 8, 9–10, 11, 13, 16, 17, 25, 34, 39, 42–43, 47, 48, 56, 59, 61, 62, 82

Fraxinetum, 115

Fredegar, 69, 71

Freedom, 24–25

Frisia and the Frisians, 20, 49, 50, 51, 62, 81, 82, 92, 96, 99, 112

Gaetica (Jordanes), 33

Garigliano, 115

Gascony, 16, 78, 81, 82, 127, 157

Gaul, 9, 11, 16, 17, 21, 22, 27–28, 33, 34, 36, 48, 50, 61, 69–70, 73, 103

Genoa and the Genoese, 41, 152

Gerbert of Rheims, 142, 158, 160, 161–62

Germanic law codes, 70

Germany and the Germans, 7, 8, 10, 11, 13, 20, 22–23, 24, 31, 34, 43, 51, 59, 61, 62, 64, 81, 82, 92, 96, 99, 100, 109, 111, 114, 123, 126, 127, 140–42, 147, 152, 157, 161, 163–64

Gildas, 34

Gnupa, 114

Gokstad ship, 98, 109

Gold coinage, 17, 20, 50–51, 57, 80, 85, 88, 93, 122, 150

Goths, 83

Gotland, 92, 109

Greece, 79, 84, 86, 89, 119, 125

Greek Church, 25–26, 62, 66, 102–3, 119, 155–56, 159; Caesaropapism in, 26–27; iconoclasm, problem of, 85–86; impact of invasions on, 129–31; schism with Rome, 86, 101, 128, 129

Greek fire, 56

Greenland, 98, 110, 112, 154

Gregory I, Pope, 66

Gregory of Tours, 69, 71, 73, 74

Gregory the Great, Pope, 30, 43, 61, 63, 64, 65, 66, 68, 128, 133

Guthram, King, 129

Hebrides, 112

Henry, Duke of Saxony, 140

Henry III, Emperor, 159

Heraclius, Emperor, 41, 42, 60, 63, 67

Heresy, 25, 26, 27, 63, 101, 102. *See also* Adoptionist heresy; Arianism; Iconoclasm; Monothelitism; Nestorianism

Hincmar of Rheims, Archbishop, 128, 131

Hungary and the Hungarians, 8-9, 10, 12, 20, 45, 111, 114, 117-18, 120, 123, 140, 142, 146, 147, 150, 156

Iceland, 98, 112, 147

Iconoclasm, 101, 102, 107, 115, 119, 129, 130

Industrial development, 50, 57, 93-96, 151, 152

Invasions, Age of (840-911), 111-16; economic impact of, 120-26; Moslem seafarers, 114-16, 122, 124, 125, 126, 129; political repercussions of, 116-20; Scandinavian movements, 111-14, 119-20, 122, 123, 124, 132, 134, 135; social impact of, 126-35

Ireland, 3, 6, 20, 29, 31, 35, 49, 50, 61, 100, 104, 112, 114, 118, 122, 123, 135, 145, 147, 150, 151, 157

Irene, Empress, 86, 87, 101, 102, 103

Isaurian law code, 107

Isidore of Seville, 71, 72, 74

Islam, 40, 41, 47, 62, 77, 78, 113, 116

Italy and the Italians, 9, 12, 16, 17, 22, 36, 44, 48, 68, 69, 79, 81, 82, 85, 86, 88-89, 92, 99, 100, 104, 117, 119, 122, 124, 126, 127, 132, 137, 138, 141, 142, 147, 151, 154, 155, 162, 166

Jelling Stone, 157

Jewelry, 37, 109

Jews, 89, 96, 122, 147, 150, 151, 152, 160

John of Biclar, 71

John of Damascus, 107

Joshua Roll, 164

Judaism, 62, 102

Julian of Toledo, 71

Justinian, Emperor, 9, 16, 17, 20, 21, 22, 28, 30, 31, 35, 39, 42, 48, 63, 68

Justinian Code, 32, 33, 107, 133

Jutland peninsula, 114, 123, 154

Kazaria and the Kazars, 40, 45-46, 47, 48, 62, 77, 79, 80, 88, 91-92, 102, 113, 120, 122, 139

Kiev, 113, 122, 123, 147, 164

Kievan Russia (911-1000), 139-40, 156, 163

Landowners, 83, 87, 98-99, 154-55

Latin Church, 25-26, 78, 79, 96, 156-59; Carolingian Empire and (718-840), 82, 99-102; hierarchy of, independence of, 27–28; impact of invasions on, 126–29; schism with Constantinople, 86, 101, 128, 129; spread of (565–718), 61–62; triumph in the West, 63–64. *See also* Arianism; Caesaropapism; Heresy; Iconoclasm; Monasticism; Papacy

Law codes, 14, 17, 22, 23, 31–33, 44, 67–68, 69, 70, 71, 72, 75, 104, 106, 107, 133, 161

Law of the Salian Franks, 34

Laws of Ine, 72

Lecapenus, Romanus, 137, 138

Lechfeld, Battle of (955), 140

Léon, 79, 143

Leo the Isaurian, Emperor, 84, 85, 102

Leo the Wise, Emperor, 129, 133

Lewis the German, King, 116, 117

Life of St. Gerald of Aurillac, 162

Life of St. Germanus, 34

Life of St. Patrick, 34

Literature, Christian, in the West, 33–34

Llewellyn the Great, 145

Lombard Code of Laws, 44, 69, 104

Lombardy and the Lombards, 8, 10, 12, 39, 41, 44, 47, 59, 63, 66, 69, 78, 79, 81, 82, 86, 97, 104, 108, 109, 125, 134, 141, 162, 163

Lorraine, 117, 140, 157

Lothaire, King, 116–17, 128

Lotharingia, 117

Louis the Pious, Emperor, 80, 81, 82, 83, 84, 93, 100, 101, 106, 110, 116

Low Countries, 49, 50, 122, 123, 151. *See also* Belgium

Luidprand, King, 104, 162

Macedonia, 89, 125

Magyars, 9, 111, 114, 117, 118, 123, 125, 127, 140, 156

Malta, 115, 121

Manuscript illuminations, 109, 164

Marculf, 70–71

Marseilles, 51, 152

Martel, Charles, 81, 82, 103

Martin, Pope, 64

Maurice, Emperor, 41, 42, 56, 60, 133, 138

Merobaudes, 37

Merovingians, 42, 43, 70, 78, 82, 83, 96, 103, 153

Metal work, 37

Methodius, St., 62, 130, 131, 156

Middle class, development of, 153, 154

Middle East, 151

Miezko, King, 140, 146

Milan, 124

Militarism, 86–87, 125–26, 155

Moimir, 118

Monasticism and monasteries, 28–31, 55, 61–62, 69, 71, 85–86, 97, 104, 107, 126–28, 130, 131–32, 157–58, 159; growth of, 64–65, 100

Money economies, 17–21, 57, 80, 85, 88, 89, 93, 120–21, 122, 123, 150

Monophysitism, 26, 63

Monothelitism, 62, 63–64, 65, 66, 67, 69

Monte Cassino, 28, 30, 64, 69, 100, 132

Moors, 71, 76, 89, 103, 163

Moravia, 80, 118, 120, 130, 131, 146, 156

Moslems, 46, 54, 77, 81, 84, 87, 88, 89–90, 96, 97, 111, 114, 119, 120, 121, 142–44, 147, 151, 152, 160, 166; invasion by, 114–16, 122, 124, 125, 126, 129

Mount Athos, 159

Music, church, 106, 133

Naples, 88, 121, 124, 150, 151

Narses, 23

Navarre, 79

Near East, 77

Nestorianism, 26, 27

Neustria, 43, 81

Neustrian Chronicle, 71

Nicephorus, Emperor, 87, 133

Nicholas I, Pope, 128, 132

Ninian, St., 29

Nithard, 131

Nordic art, 109

Normandy, 112, 146, 151

North Africa, 40, 41, 77, 90, 115, 121, 124, 151

North Sea, 81, 112, 114, 122

Norway and the Norwegians, 92, 93, 114, 145, 157

Notitia Dignitatum, 14

Novellae, 17

Novgorod, 113

Odo, St., 162

Offa of Marcia, 79–80, 93

Ogham stones, 35, 37, 74

Oleg, 113

Olga, Empress, 156

Ommayed caliphs, 116, 142–44

Orosius, 33, 132

Oseberg ship, 109

Ostrogoths, 7, 9, 11, 13, 16, 20, 23, 63

Otto I, Emperor, 140–41, 158

Otto II, Emperor, 141, 142

Otto III, Emperor, 141, 142

Ottonian Empire (911–1000), 140–42, 157, 161, 164

Ottonian Renaissance, 161

Paganism, 31, 61, 102, 127, 155, 156, 157, 166

Papacy, 26–27, 30, 61, 63–64, 65–67, 68–69, 78, 79, 82, 85, 86, 101–2, 119, 128, 129, 132, 141, 142, 158–59, 166

Papal States, 101

Patrick, St., 29

Paul the Deacon, 69, 105, 106

Pavia, 44, 69, 104, 124

Peasants, 98, 125, 155

Pepin, 81, 82, 86, 93, 101, 103, 117

Persia, 41, 51, 60, 91

Phocas, Nicephorus, 137, 138

Photius, Patriarch, 128, 129, 133

Piracy and pirates, 21, 111–12, 115, 122, 124, 125, 152

Plato, 32, 133, 162–63

Poland, 140, 142, 146, 150, 156

Polytype of Abbot Irminon, 97

Political patterns, new, 9–11

Population movements, 11–13

Procopius, 32, 35, 67

Protofeudalism, 59

Provence, 81, 115, 117, 125, 127, 132, 146, 152, 153, 157

Psellus, 163

Radislav, 118

Ravenna, 32, 33, 36, 66, 86

Religious changes (565–718), 61–67

Rhinelands, 10, 12, 13, 15, 51, 57, 62, 96, 97, 122, 123, 147

Rhodian Sea Law, 67–68

Roman Empire, 3–4; architecture in (400–565), 35–36; art in (400–565), 36–37; Christian literature in, 33–34; Church in (400–565), 25–31; culture in (400–565), 31–37; decline of, 5–6; economic developments (400–565), 11–21, (565–718), 47–57; as Great Power (565–718), 39, 41–42; political power, problems of, 7–11; secular and religious culture in (565–718), 68–73; social relations and interrelations (400–565), 22–25. *See also* Eastern Roman Empire

Roman Europe, 3–4; political power, problems of, 7–11

Romania, 7

Rome, 36, 63, 66, 68, 73, 78, 86, 104, 108, 127, 128, 129, 141

Roswitha, 161

Royal Annals, 106

Rule of St. Benedict, 30, 100

Runic writing, 34–35

Rurik, 113

Russia, 3, 8, 9, 20, 50, 51, 77, 80, 92, 110, 113–14, 120, 131, 136, 139–40, 147, 156. *See also* Kievan Russia

Russian Primary Chronicle, 113

"Saints' Lives," 34, 67, 70, 71, 72, 133, 162

Salin, Edouard, 21, 37, 74

Salonika, 88, 89, 122, 130

Salvian, 34

Samo, 40, 47, 80

Santiago de Compostela, 143

Sardinia, 115

Saxons, *see* Anglo-Saxons

Saxony, 78, 81, 99

Scandinavia and the Scandinavians, 3, 7, 8, 10, 20, 34, 37, 39–40, 46, 47, 48, 49, 50, 51, 59, 76, 80, 98, 109, 110, 119–20, 136, 142, 145, 152, 154, 157; invasions by, 111–14, 119–20, 122, 123, 124, 132, 134, 135. *See also* Denmark; Norway; Sweden; Vikings

Scotland and the Scots, 3, 12, 13, 20, 61, 118, 145

Scotus, John, 131

Seigneurial system, impact of invasions on, 125–26. *See also* Landowners

Septimania, 43, 78, 81, 96, 122

Serbs, 131, 146, 156

Seville, 163

Shipbuilding, 98, 154

Sicily, 87, 88, 115, 119, 121, 122, 124, 137, 151

Sidonius Appolinaris, 17, 28, 32

Silk industry, 57

Silver coinage, 17, 20, 51, 57, 89, 93, 120–21

Sköttkonung, Olaf, 145

Slavs, 8, 12, 13, 41, 47, 59, 62, 76, 78, 79, 84, 91, 102, 117, 118, 120, 129, 130, 131, 141, 142, 147, 156, 159

Social developments, 22–25, 58–60, 154–59

Spain and the Spaniards, 9, 10, 16, 17, 22, 31, 33, 40, 47, 48, 49, 51, 71, 73, 76, 77, 78, 79, 89–90, 92, 93, 96, 97, 100, 103, 115, 121, 122, 125, 127, 136, 151, 155, 160, 163, 164, 166

Spanish March, 78, 81, 82, 96

Stephen, St., 146

Stirrup, the, 56, 59, 97

Suevians, 7

Sutton Hoo treasure, 21, 49, 74

Sviatoslav, Tsar, 139, 156

Sweden and the Swedes, 12, 46, 50, 74, 80, 92, 93, 100, 112, 114, 128, 145, 157

Swords, pattern-welded, 57, 97

Sylvester II, Pope, 158

Syria, 9, 26, 41, 77, 88, 121, 137, 151

Technological developments, 56–57, 97–98, 154

Tervel, 80

Thematibus, De, 163

Theodoric, Emperor, 16, 28, 32; Edict of, 33

Theodosian Code, 14, 23, 31

Theodosius, Emperor, 3

Theophanes, 133

Thomas the Slav, 87, 89

Thrace, 89

Toledo, 90

Towns, 14–15, 16, 48, 51, 55

Trade and trade routes, 20, 46, 48–49, 54, 88–89, 91–92, 93–96, 113, 114, 120–24, 138–39, 147–53, 155

Tryggvason, Olaf, 157

Turkestan, 46, 90, 91

Ulfilas, 7

University of Constantinople, 163

Uppsala, 80, 114, 128

Urban development, patterns of, 13–17

Utrecht Psalter, 109

Valencia, 90, 143

Vandals, 7, 9, 11, 21, 63

Varangians, 110, 113–14

Venice and the Venetians, 54, 79, 81, 88, 92, 96, 115, 121, 124, 138–39, 141, 142, 150, 151, 152, 162, 163

Vikings, 81, 82, 84, 98, 100, 111–12, 115, 117, 119–20, 122, 123, 124, 132, 145, 157

Villas, 15–17

Visigothic law codes, 23, 71

Visigoths, 5, 6, 7, 10, 11, 13, 16, 25, 28, 39, 41, 43–44, 47, 56, 59, 104, 105

Vladimir, St., 139, 156

Wales, 145

Warships, 154

Weaving techniques, 57

Western Church, *see* Latin Church

West Francia, 116, 117, 126

Westmoreland, 112

Widefathom, Ivar, 46

Zeno, Emperor, 26

Zimisces, John, 137, 138, 139, 159

A Note on the Type

The text of this book is set in Electra, a typeface designed by W(illiam) A(ddison) Dwiggins for the Mergenthaler Linotype Company and first made available in 1935. Electra cannot be classified as either "modern or "old style." It is not based on any historical model, and hence does not echo any particular period or style of type design. It avoids the extreme contrast between "thick" and "thin" elements that marks most modern faces, and is without eccentricities which catch the eye and interfere with reading. In general, Electra is a simple, readable typeface which attempts to give a feeling of fluidity, power, and speed.

W. A. Dwiggins (1880–1956) was born in Martinsville, Ohio, and studied art in Chicago. In 1904 he moved to Hingham, Massachusetts, where he built a solid reputation as a designer of advertisements and as a calligrapher. He began an association with the Mergenthaler Linotype Company in 1929, and over the next twenty-seven years designed a number of book types, of which Metro, Electra, and Caledonia have been used very widely. In 1930 Dwiggins became interested in marionettes, and through the years made many important contributions to the art of puppetry and the design of marionettes.

Composed, printed, and bound by The Colonial Press, Inc., Clinton, Mass. Typography by Leon Bolognese.